LEARN TO SPEAK
NORWEGIAN
(WITHOUT EVEN TRYING)

Stephen Hernandez

Learn to speak Spanish (without even trying)

Really helpful tips on how to learn to speak Spanish it is money very well spent.

(Kindle Customer)

Learn to speak German (without even trying)

Learn to speak German is a super addition to this series of books from an author whose love of languages shines through in his writing.

(Amazon Reader)

Learn to speak French (without even trying)

5 Star!

(Amazon Reader)

Learn to speak Portuguese (without even trying)

5 out of 5 stars!

(Amazon Reader)

For the Viking in all of us

A new language is a new life.

—PERSIAN PROVERB

CONTENTS

LEARNING NORWEGIAN

The purpose of this book is to teach you *how* to learn, rather than what to learn. It would be impossible to discuss the Norwegian language's complete grammatical structure and, every Norwegian word and its correct pronunciation in one book and if ever such a book were written it would be incredibly tedious. The aim of this book is to get you speaking Norwegian to the extent you can hold a reasonable conversation with a native speaker and you can read and understand a newspaper and magazine article written in Norwegian. Once you have progressed that far you will not need the help of any book, course, or teacher—you will just need to practice.

Make no mistake—learning a language when you are not living in a country where it is spoken is very difficult. Not only do you not have situations where you can practice your new found learning but you are constantly bombarded by your native language as soon as you leave the classroom or your chosen place of learning. In many ways it becomes a case of perseverance. I liken it to the starting of a new exercise regime. You enroll in a local gym (giving you the added incentive that you are actually paying to get fitter). At first you are full of enthusiasm and energy so you set yourself unrealistic goals. Instead of starting off walking and progressing to running, you start off at a mad sprint and quickly tire. The novelty soon wears off and going to the gym becomes an irksome duty. Then excuses for not going begin to kick in, and before you know it you have given up altogether.

- Absolutely anyone can learn Norwegian.
- I'm completely serious.

It doesn't matter what your excuse is. Maybe you think you stink at languages. Maybe you think you're too lazy. Maybe you flunked out of high school Norwegian (if it exists!) or maybe you just can't pronounce Norwegian words no matter how hard you try.

If you really want to learn Norwegian, **you can do it.** Best of all you can do it without even trying. The only effort you have to make is to read this book (and even then you can skip the bits you don't like), make a concrete plan to study (one you can stick to), keep it fun (extremely important), and stay motivated over the long haul (self-explanatory).

- Decide on a simple, attainable goal to start with so that you don't feel overwhelmed.
- Make learning Norwegian a lifestyle change.

- Invite Norwegian into your daily life. That way, your brain will consider it something useful and worth caring about.
- Let technology help you out. The internet is absolutely great for learning Norwegian—use it.
- Think about learning Norwegian as a gateway to new experiences. Think of the fun things you want to do and turn them into language-learning opportunities.
- Make new friends. Interacting in Norwegian is key—it will teach you to intuitively express your thoughts, instead of mentally translating each sentence before you say it. If you are a bit shy about getting the ball rolling with native speakers nearby, you can do this online (there is a whole chapter on this).
- Most of all do not worry about making mistakes. One of the most common barriers to conversing in a new language is the fear of making mistakes. But native speakers are like doting parents: any attempt from you to communicate in their language is objective proof that you are some sort of gifted genius. They'll appreciate your effort and even help you. The more you speak, the closer you'll get to the elusive ideal of "native fluency."

To start off with don't set yourself unrealistic goals or a grandiose study plan. Keep it simple. Set aside a small amount of time that you can reasonably spare even if it just means getting up 15 minutes earlier in the morning. If you set that time aside and avoid distractions that 15 minutes will be invaluable. Above all make it as fun as possible. No one said learning a new language was easy but neither should it be irksome.

You can use this book in tandem with any other learning resource you may be using at the moment if that resource is working for you. At some point, though, you will find you have your particular way of learning, and discovering that is very important. Once you find what works, you will have achieved an important milestone, and your learning will accelerate accordingly. I hope that with this book you will find your "way" sooner rather than later. That is what I designed it to do.

This book has no strict order (you can jump to and from chapters if you want), no particular rules to follow, and I definitely do not take anything for granted except the fact that you want to learn to speak Norwegian and most probably want the experience to be as painless as possible.

I want to make it clear once again (as it is important), that this book is not designed to "teach" you Norwegian. It is designed to help you learn how to teach yourself to speak Norwegian with the least effort possible—hence, the sub-title: "without even trying". It gives you a process and pointers on how to learn Norwegian effectively and easily. Consider it an autodidactic guide.

It is also a guide to learning subconsciously. By subconsciously, I do not mean that you go to sleep listening to tapes in Norwegian or practice some kind of self-hypnosis. What we are aiming at is picking up Norwegian without forcing the issue. The greatest aim in learning any language is being able to think in that language and not be aware that you are doing it. Then, you speak automatically without over thinking the process. Stick with me and you will obtain that goal.

Sound impossible? It won't be by the time you have finished this book.

A journey of a thousand miles begins with a single step.

Yeah, we've all heard that one from a thousand language teachers.

As far as advice goes, that saying is about as useful as an ashtray on a motorbike.

Think about it. If you're stranded in a foreign wilderness with no idea about *how* to get where you want to go, you'll have an extraordinarily difficult time getting there no matter how many footsteps you take. In fact, you'll probably end up going around in circles.

But if you've got a map and compass, as well as some decent navigating skills, you're likely to be on your way a lot faster.

In the same way, when you're starting to learn a new language, it helps to have a road map to both guide you along and guarantee that you're still headed in the right direction when you get stuck or feel lost.

Just like physical maps, a map for language learning should be based on what other people have seen. There are a number of polyglots and dedicated language learners out there who have become cartographers of the linguistic frontier. We will be drawing on their collective experience.

We will take this collective language learning experience, along with some scientific and technical know-how, and set out on the path to learning a new language in double time.

Here are some basic strategies to get you started:

- Become your own coach—develop goals and strategies. If you have heard of bullet journals, now is a good time to put one into practice. If this fails to ring the smallest of bells in the lockers of your memory, Google it and decide if you like the idea—it comes in very handy when learning a new language.

- A lot of the time, when we start something new, we make vague statements like, "I want to be able to speak well as quickly as possible," or, "I'm going to study Norwegian as much as I possibly can." This can be a problem because, when we create such vague goals, it can be very difficult to achieve any sort of meaningful result. That's why orienting your Norwegian learning odyssey should start with the use of two techniques: **SMART goals** and **metacognitive strategies**.

- **SMART,** in this case, is an acronym that means **S**pecific, **M**easurable, **A**chievable, **R**esults, **T**ime-bound. The synopsis of this is that you need to make really, really concrete goals that can be achieved (even if you're incredibly lazy—see next chapter). Setting realistic goals like this is an essential skill for anyone studying by themselves, as well as anyone who wishes to maximize their study time.

- **Metacognitive strategies** involves three steps. First, you plan. Ask yourself what your specific goals are and what strategies you're going to use to achieve them. Second, start learning and keep track of how well you do every day. Are you having problems that need new solutions? Write that down. Are you consistently succeeding or failing in a certain area? Keep track of that, too. And the third and final step, after a few weeks to a month, it is time to **evaluate yourself**. Were you able to achieve your goals? If not, why? What strategies did and didn't work? Then the whole process repeats again.

These two techniques naturally fit together quite well, and they're both indispensable for making sure you're cooking with gas every time you sit or lie down to study.

Total immersion (i.e., living in a Norwegian speaking country) and speaking, seeing, hearing, reading and writing it all the time is, of course, the ultimate way to learn and is certainly the ultimate goal to strive for. Most of us aren't free to move from country to country as we please and must make decisions about when the best time would be for us to go to that oh-so-wonderful country we've been daydreaming about for countless hours. So, this book is aimed mainly at people who are studying from home in their native country but also has a large travel section for before you travel.

The Internet

Throughout this book, I'll suggest links to websites worth visiting for more information. I assume that their content is legal and correct, but I have no way of knowing, and accept no responsibility for them. site owners change the content all the time, web pages get deleted and sites close down in the blink of an eye. If you find an inappropriate or dead link, let me know. you'll find my e-mail address at the end of the book or on my website.

Enjoy yourself.

Languages can be difficult to master. Even the easiest of languages for English speakers can take six hundred hours to conquer, according to the Foreign Service Institute, and perhaps much more than that if you want to do something with it professionally. This is not something you can do day in, day out without getting some pleasure out of the whole *ordeal.*

Thankfully, language is as human an obstacle as it gets and is naturally tied to amazing and fulfilling rewards. Think about how wonderful it is or could be to read your favorite Norwegian author in the original, or understand a Norwegian film without having to look at the sub-titles, or most amazing of all, hold a conversation with someone in their native language! Language is the thing that connects us to other people and the social benefits are extremely powerful.

Just think about how often you check Facebook. Why are social networking sites so popular? Because any information connected to other people is inherently seductive. So, from the get-go, make sure that you use your language skills for what they were made for—socializing.

Sometimes, when your schedule is crazy, you'll be tempted to jettison the "fun" things that made you attracted to learning Norwegian in the first place to get some regular practice in. Maybe you'll skip your favorite Norwegian TV show because you can't understand it without subtitles yet (more on this later), or you'll forget to keep up with the latest news on your favorite Norwegian singer or band.

Make time for the things that got you started. They're what motivate you and push you through when language learning seems like a brutal punishment.

Really, it's all about balance. The steps are all here, laid out for you.

Only by starting out on the journey will you gain intuitive control, the sense of masterful dexterity like that of a professional athlete or a samurai warrior.

You have your map.

Now you just need to take those first steps ...

CHAPTER ONE

LEARNING AT HOME
(even if you're really lazy)

Do you have hopes and dreams of speaking a language fluently, but you're too lazy to study?

So do many people, but they give up before they've even started because it just seems like so much effort towards an intangible goal. And seriously—who *wants* to study?

But what if I told you that your laziness, far from being a limitation, could actually make you great at learning Norwegian?

Read on (if you can be bothered) to find out why the lazy way is often the best way and learn ways you can leverage your laziness to learn a language effectively at home.

Lazy people find better ways to do things

If you were a builder at the end of the 19th century, life was hard. Long hours. Bad pay. Little regard for health and safety. If you were really unlucky, it could even cost you your life: five men died during the construction of the Empire State

Building, and 27 died working on the Brooklyn Bridge. Mortality rates amongst builders in Victorian Britain were even more horrendous. In short, being a builder was a dangerous job.

What qualities did builders need in such a demanding and dangerous job?

Tenacity? Diligence? Stamina?

No. Not at all.

In 1868, a young construction worker named Frank Gilbreth, while observing colleagues to understand why some bricklayers were more effective than others, made a startling discovery.

The best builders weren't those who tried the hardest. The men Gilbreth learned the most from were the laziest ones.

Laying bricks requires repeating the same skilled movements over and over again: the fewer motions, the better. In an attempt to conserve energy, the "lazy" builders had found ways to lay bricks with a minimum number of motions. In short, they'd found more effective ways to get the job done.

But what do lazy bricklayers have to do with learning Norwegian, apart from the fact that I worked as one for a while? (I wasn't very good at laying bricks, but I was excellent at being lazy!)

Well, inspired by his lazy colleagues, Gilbreth went on to pioneer "time and motion study," a technique that streamlines work systems and is still used today in many fields to increase productivity. You know that person in the operating room who passes scalpels to the surgeon and wipes their brow? Gilbreth came up with that idea.

Hiring someone to pass you things from 20 centimeters away and wipe the sweat off your own forehead? It doesn't get much lazier than that. Yet it helps surgeons work more efficiently and probably saves lives in the process.

The bottom line? The lazy way is usually the smartest way.

Over the years, Gilbreth's ideas have been attributed to people like Bill Gates, who is (falsely) reported to have said: "I will always choose a lazy person to do a difficult job because he will find an easy way to do it." (This attribution, although factually incorrect, makes a nice motivational poster to hang in your office.)

The lazy way

One of the most embarrassing episodes in my life (and there are quite a few, believe me!) was when I unadvisedly went to a parents' evening at my young daughter's primary school. The teacher asked each child in turn what their fathers did for a living. My daughter's response: "He lies on the sofa with his hands down his trousers."

Actually, that is partly true, although you may be relieved to know that I don't spend *all* my time with my hands down my trousers. If there's one thing I love more than writing, listening to the radio, and browsing the web, it's sitting or lying on the sofa in my pants, reading or watching TV—a lot of the time in Norwegian. Fortunately, with regards to writing this book, these activities aren't mutually exclusive, so I'm always on the lookout for ways to combine my favorite pastimes.

I've scoured the web to find the best resources to learn Norwegian, and this book contains my findings. Hopefully, the information contained herein will save you a lot of time and money spent on useless systems and pointless exercises and will repay your faith in me. When you speak Norwegian (which you will), please remember to recommend it to your friends. Even if you don't use a computer, there is enough basic information here to get you started on your path to learning Norwegian. But I would strongly advise getting on the internet if you intend to learn from home with some degree of success.

If your school was anything like mine, you may have some experience learning languages with the "try harder" approach: page after page of grammar exercises, long vocabulary lists, listening exercises about stationary or some other excruciatingly boring topic. And if you still can't speak the language after all that effort? Well, you should try harder.

But what if there's a better way to learn a language? A lazier way, that you can use to learn a language at home and, with less effort?

A way to learn by doing things you actually enjoy? A way to learn by having a laugh with native speakers? A way to learn without taking your pajamas off?

There is.

Don't get me wrong. Languages take time and effort; there's no getting around that. This isn't about being idle.

It's about finding effective ways to learn (remember: SMART and metacognitive strategies?) so you can stop wasting time and energy on stuff that doesn't work. With that in mind, I've put together a collection of lazy (but highly effective) ways to learn a language at home or away.

They'll help you:

- Speak a language better by studying less!
- Go against "traditional" language learning methods to get better results.
- Get fluent in a language while sitting around in your undies and drinking beer (this isn't compulsory).

Don't study (much).

A lot of people try to learn a language by "studying." They try really hard to memorize grammar rules and vocabulary in the hope that one day, all the pieces will come together and they'll magically start speaking the language.

Sorry, but languages don't work that way. Trying to speak a language by doing grammar exercises is like trying to make bread by reading cookbooks. Sure, you'll pick up some tips, but you'll never learn how to bake unless you're willing to get your hands dirty.

Languages are a learn-by-doing kind of a deal. The best way to learn to speak, understand, read, and write a language is by practicing speaking, listening, reading, and writing. That doesn't mean you should never study grammar or vocabulary. It helps to get an idea of how the language works. But if you dedicate a disproportionate amount of time to that stuff, it'll clutter your learning experience and hold you back from actually speaking Norwegian.

You'll learn much faster by *using the language.*

Now, if you're totally new to language learning, you may be wondering how you can start using a language you don't know yet. If you're learning completely from scratch, a good textbook can help you pick up the basics. But avoid ones that teach lots of grammar rules without showing you how to use them in real life. The best textbooks are the ones that give you lots of example conversations and introduce grammar in bite-size pieces.

As soon as you can, aim to get lots of exposure to the Norwegian language being used in a real way. If you're a lower-level learner, you can start by reading books that have been simplified for your level (called graded readers). Look for ones accompanied by audio so you can work on your listening at the same time. If you can, keep a diary or journal of your experience with different methods of learning. Bullet journals are great for this. Never heard of them? They are basically a sort of a cross between a diary and a to-do list. Keeping one will help you see what works for you and what doesn't, and also to chart your progress. You can buy readymade ones to suit you or design your own. You can use it for motivation when you feel like you are getting nowhere, as you will see at a glance all the progress you have made. Believe me, you will be surprised at how far you have come and sometimes you just need a little reminder to give you that motivational push. You will also be able to see what areas you need to improve in and the types of things you are best at. When you are feeling low, go back to the stuff you are best at.

Consider how a child has learned to speak a language. Presumably, unless it was a precocious genius, it did not start off by reading a primer in grammar. Children start off by observing and identifying. Naming and pronunciation comes from hearing the description of the object from others, usually adults, or other kids fluent in the language.

A note on written Norwegian: Nynorsk and Bokmål

Nynorsk is one of the two written standards of the Norwegian language, the other being Bokmål. Nynorsk was established in1929 as one of the two state-sanctioned fusions of Ivar

Aasen's (Norwegian philologist) standard Norwegian language with the Dano-Norwegian language, the other such fusion being the aforementioned Bokmål.

Post-it Notes

There is something you can do right now, right this minute. Start off by naming in Norwegian the objects that surround you, write the Norwegian name for the object on a Post-it Note, and stick it on the object. You can find the Norwegian translation for any household object online or in a two-way dictionary. I would advise using an online dictionary if you can, as these usually include a guide to pronunciation that you can actually listen to without trying to do it phonetically.

Put the Post-it Note at eye level or some place you will encounter it immediately upon looking at the object. Begin by saying the objects name out loud—,or perhaps, if you have company, in your head. At this point, don't worry too much if your friends and family think you have gone a little crazy. You are learning a new language; they are not. Give yourself a pat on the back instead.

Below is a short list of some common things around the house to give you a start and the idea behind this method. Remember to write the name of the object in **Norwegian** only. Preferably, put your Post-it Note on an immovable object (your spouse or significant other might take exception to having a Post-it Note stuck on their forehead, and so might your dog or cat).

- Put the Post it Notes on everything in your house (use a two-way dictionary). It is a great way to learn nouns (the name of things). Don't forget to put if they are feminine, masculine or neuter (they are in brackets) and we will be touching on them later. Soon you will begin to identify these objects in Norwegian without consciously thinking about it.

Kitchen

gaffel (n) masc	fork
vannkoker (n) masc	kettle
tallerken (n) masc	plate
kniv (n) masc	knife
kjele (n) masc	pot
skje (n) fem	spoon
stekepanne (n) fem	frying pan
skjærebrett (n) neut	cutting board
bolle (n) masc	bowl
vask (n) (masc)	kitchen sink

You can listen to an audio of these words and following phrases to practice your Norwegian listening and pronunciation at: norwegianclass101.com (https://www.norwegianclass101.com/norwegian-vocabulary-lists/kitchen/)

Kitchen phrases

rød vannkoker	red kettle

gaffel på en tallerken   fork on a plate

Kan du gi meg kniven?   Could you pass me the knife?

den kjelen er ti år gammel   that pot is ten years old

flytende medisin, en skje og en liten plastikk kopp
liquid medicine , a spoon and a small plastic cup

Løken blir sautert i stekepanna. The onions are being sautéed
in the frying pan.

Kokken deler et hardkokt egg på et skjærebrett. The cook is
cutting a hard-boiled egg on the cutting board.

blå bolle   blue bowl

General home items and misc

et søppelspann   a garbage can

ei inngangsdør   a front door

sengetøy   bedding

tepper   carpets

puter   pillows

håndkler   towels

gardiner	curtains
bilder	pictures
lamper	lamps
ei stue	a living room
et soverom	a bedroom
et kjøkken	a kitchen
et toalett	a toilet
en enebolig	a cottage
en leilighet	an apartment
et gjerde	a fence
en lekeplass	a playground
en garsaje	a garage
ei takrenne	a gutter
el trapp	a staircase
en garderobe	a wardrobe
en ovn	an oven

å eie	to own
å leie	to rent
å flytte	to move

Phrases—General Home

Jeg flytter til et nytt hus.	I am moving to a new house.
Jeg eier en pen enebolig.	I own a nice house.
Du kan leie et lite rekkehus.	You can rent a small row house.
Huset mitt har to toaletter.	My house has two toilets.
Gå ned trappa til kjøkkenet.	Go down the stairs to the kitchen.
Jeg bor i en stor leilighet.	I live in a big apartment
Det har et soverom og et bad.	It has a bedroom and a bathroom.
i et rom	in a room
i et hus	in a house
i en hage	in a garden

et soverom	a bedroom
ei seng	a bed
et skap	a cupboard
ei pute	a pillow
ei dyne	a mattress
et kjøleskap	a refrigerator
et kjøkkenbord	a kitchen table
en komfyr	an oven
en vask	a wash basin
et bad	a bathroom
en do	a commode
en dusj	a shower
et speil	a mirror
ei stue	a living room
et salongbord	a coffee table
en sofa	a sofa

en lenestol	a chair
ei bokhylle	a book rack
gardiner	curtains
en hage	a garden
blomster	flowers
et tre	a tree
en terrasse	a terrace
hagemøbler	garden furniture

Norwegian Definite Articles

You may not have learned this at school, but in English the word "the" is called a definite article. That is because the word "the" points to a very specific thing. For example, you may tell someone, "I want the book," assuming that they will bring you the book you have in mind.

However, if you tell them, "I want a book," you will get whatever book they choose to hand you! That is because the words "a" or "an" or "some" are indefinite articles and point to a general group of items, things, people or places.

Norwegian is unusual in that the definite article, i.e. the, is formed by adding -en at the end of the masculine words, -a at the end of neuter words.

Norwegian Nouns and Articles

How to say a, an, the, this, that, these and those in Norwegian

Nouns

Nouns in Norwegian (Bokmål) have two genders, masculine and neuter, which adjectives must agree with when modifying nouns. Technically there is a third gender, feminine (which Nynorsk retains), but since feminine nouns can be written as masculine nouns, I'm including feminine nouns in the masculine category.

There are two indefinite articles (a or an) that correspond with these genders: en for masculine nouns and et for neuter nouns. In the vocabulary lists, a noun followed by (n) means that it is a neuter noun and it takes the indefinite article **et**. The majority of nouns in Norwegian are masculine, so they take the indefinite article **en**.

The definite article (the) is not a separate word like in most other languages. It is simply a form of the indefinite article **attached to the end of the noun**. Note that en words ending in a vowel retain that vowel and add an -n instead of adding -en. And et words ending in -e just add -t. Furthermore, the t of et as an indefinite article is pronounced; however, the t is silent in the definite article -et attached to the noun. (For feminine nouns, the indefinite article is **ei** and the definite article that is attached to the noun is **-a**. In theory, this gender does still exist in Bokmål, but in practice, it is rarely used and the feminine nouns are inflected like masculine nouns, i.e. add -en instead of -a for the definite form.)

En words (masculine)

Indefinite		Definite	
en fisk	a fish	fisken	the fish
en baker	a baker	bakeren	the baker
en hage	a garden	hagen	the garden

Et words (neuter)

Indefinite		Definite	
et vindu	a window	vinduet	the window
et barn	a child	barnet	the child
et hus	a house	huset	the house

Demonstrative Adjectives

masculine	denne dressen	this suit	den dressen	that suit
neuter	dette skjerfet	this scarf	det skjerfet	that scarf
plural	disse skoene	these shoes	de skoene	those shoes

Notice that the noun that follows a demonstrative adjective must have the definite article attached to it. (The feminine form of demonstratives is identical to the masculine; **denne** and **den**.)

The only case of nouns that is used in Norwegian is the genitive (showing possession), and it is easily formed by adding an -s to the noun. This is comparable to adding -'s in English to show possession. However, if the noun already ends in -s, then you add nothing (unlike English where we add -' or -'s).

Olavs hus - Olav's house

Sit around in your undies (just like The Naked Trader!)
Next, you'll need to practice speaking. Luckily, you can now do this on Skype, so you only need to get dressed from the waist up.

The best place for online conversation classes is italki (italki.com) Here, you can book one-on-one conversation lessons with native speakers called community tutors.

Talking to native speakers

This is, by far, the best way to learn a foreign language, but there's one problem with this method that no one talks about.

To start with, those native speakers everyone is going on about may not want to talk to you.

When you start speaking a foreign language, it's all mind blanks, silly mistakes, and sounding like a two-year-old, which makes communication slow and awkward.

It's not you that's the problem. You have to go through that stage if you want to speak a foreign language.
But you need the right people to practice with. Supportive ones who encourage you to speak and don't make you feel embarrassed when you get stuck or make mistakes.

The best place to find these people?

The internet.

The fastest (and most enjoyable way) to learn a language is with regular, one-on-one speaking practice. Online tutors are perfect because it's so easy to work with them—you can do a lesson whenever it suits you and from wherever you have an internet connection, which makes it simple to stick to regular lessons.

Let's just run through how to sign up with italki, although the procedure is much the same with other online sites:
- Go to italki.com.
- Fill in your details, including which language you're learning.
- Once you get to the main italki screen, you'll see your profile with your upcoming lessons. At the moment, it says zero, so let's go ahead and set one up.
- Click on "find a teacher."

- Here, you'll find filters like "price," "availability," and "specialties." Set these to fit in with your budget, schedule, and learning goals.
- Explore the teacher profiles and watch the introduction videos to find a teacher you'll enjoy working with.
- Click on "book now," and you'll see their lesson offers.

Informal tutoring

When choosing your lessons, you'll often see "informal tutoring," which is a pure-conversation class. This kind of lesson is great value because the tutor doesn't have to prepare anything beforehand. They just join you on Skype and start chatting

Booking your first lesson

Once you've chosen the kind of lesson you'd like, choose the time that suits you, and voilà, you've just booked your first lesson with an online tutor! Well done—I know it can feel a little intimidating at first, but creating opportunities to practice is the most important thing you can do if you want to learn to speak Norwegian. Remember: practice, practice, practice. Have I stressed that enough?

The difference between professional tutors and community tutors

When choosing a teacher, you'll also see a filter called "teacher type" and the option to choose between professional teachers and community tutors. What's the difference?

Professional teachers are qualified teachers vetted by italki—they have to upload their teaching certificate to gain this title. These classes tend to be more like "classic language lessons." The teacher will take you through a structured course, preparing lessons beforehand and teaching you new grammar and vocabulary during each lesson.

Good for:

- If you're a total beginner.
- You're not sure where to start, and you'd like guidance from an expert.

Community tutors are native speakers who offer informal tutoring, where the focus is 100% on conversation skills. They'll give you their undivided attention for an hour while you try to speak, and they'll help by giving you words and corrections you need to get your point across.

Good for:

- If you've already spent some time learning the theory and you feel like you're going round in circles. You need to put it into practice. (Remember!)
- You're happy to take control of your own learning by suggesting topics and activities you'd like to try.
- You're on a budget—these classes are usually very good value.

If both of these options are out of your budget range, you can also use italki to find a language partner, which is free—you find a native speaker of the language you're learning (in this case, Norwegian, of course!) who also wants to learn your native language, and you teach each other. (You will find a lot of Norwegian speakers who want and are very willing to practice their English, believe me. You can also use your social media connections, that's what it's there for—socializing! Haven't got any Norwegian-speaking friends on Facebook? Make some.)

Important tip for finding the right tutor

Experiment with a few different tutors until you find one you click with. When you find a tutor you get along well with, they end up becoming like a friend—you'll look forward to meeting them and will be motivated to keep showing up to your lessons.

Prepare for your first lesson

Spending a little time preparing will allow you to focus during the lesson and get as much out of it as possible. These little gems of Norwegian can also be used to open a conversation with a native Norwegian speaker in any real-life situation, not just chatting online

Learn the basic pleasantries

"Hello," "goodbye," "please," "sorry," and "thank you" will take you a long way!

Learn basic communication phrases

It's important to try and speak in the language as much as possible without switching back into English. Those moments when you're scrambling for words and it feels like your brain's exploding—that's when you learn the most!

Here are some phrases to get you going (if you are not sure about pronunciation go to the chapter on Travel):

Basic Norwegian Phrases

Ja - Yes.

Nei - No

Vær så snill. - Please.

Takk. - Thank you.

Vær så god. - You're welcome.

Unnskyld. - Excuse me.

Beklager. - I am sorry.

God morgen. - Good morning.

God kveld. - Good evening.

God natt. - Good night.

Norwegian Phrases for Meeting & Greeting

Snakker du engelsk? - Do you speak English?

Finnes det noen her som snakker engelsk? - Does anyone here speak English?

Jeg snakker bare litt norsk. - I only speak a little Norwegian.

Hva heter du? - What is your name?

Jeg heter Kari. - My name is Kari.

Hvordan har du det? - How are you?

Takk, jeg har det bra. - I'm fine, thank you.

Det er så hyggelig å treffe deg. - I am very glad to meet you.

Jeg forstår ikke. - I don't understand.

Hva sa du? - What did you say?

Kan du snakke saktere? - Can you speak more slowly?

Jeg forstår det veldig godt. - I understand perfectly.

Some Norwegian Dialogue

God morgen, snakker du engelsk? - Good morning, do you speak English?

Jeg beklager, jeg snakker ikke engelsk. - I'm sorry, I do not speak English.

Dessverre snakker jeg bare litt norsk. - Unfortunately, I only speak a little Norwegian.

Det er helt i orden. Jeg forstår hva du sier. - That's all right. I understand you.

CHAPER TWO

LEARNING NORWEGIAN ON YOUR OWN

If you want to learn Norwegian independently, you're going to need a few things in your head-locker.

- Motivation (to keep going)
- Focus/Mindfulness (to be effective)
- Time/Patience (for everything to sink in)

Without these three things, it's impossible to learn a language.

There seems to be one killer rule to set yourself up for success: **keep it simple!**

With tonnes of Norwegian websites, apps, and courses out there, it can be tempting to jump from one to the next.

But there's one golden rule to remember ...

It's usually more effective to calmly work your way through one book or stick with one study method than to try different things out of curiosity. It is therefore doubly important to pick the right study methods. The best will

be referred to in this book so you don't waste your valuable study time.

The focus you'll get from this keeps self-doubt away and helps you learn more deeply.

If you are learning by yourself, for whatever reasons, you will have to *work* a little bit every day at your Norwegian to succeed. Dedicating a regular amount of time every day, no matter how little, is more productive than learning sporadically in large chunks.

You will need to spend a lot of your time listening to Norwegian. If you don't, how do you expect to ever be able to follow along in a conversation?

If you are completely new to studying and like to read, then there is a pretty neat way of starting off your Norwegian adventure with an online program called: Skapago (skapago.tachable.com) "The Mystery of Nils."

With "The Mystery of Nils" you learn through story. The story (a kind of mystery—obviously) is a coherent story, which starts very simply, but develops into a fascinating novel. Can't stop reading? Well then—you will have to learn Norwegian! In this course you will be able to read the story and listen to it as well—it is read by native Norwegian speakers.

The story is written using the most frequently used words in the Norwegian language. Separate texts and exercises focus on conversational topics that will prepare you for living in Norway. Recorded video of the vocabulary will make it easy for you to pronounce new words correctly.

It is not structured like a normal Norwegian course because the course syllabus emerges from the story.

It works like this:
Most Norwegian courses are structured by taking a bunch of grammar rules, putting them together in a certain order, and then teaching them to you one-by-one in a series of lessons.

This is dull; it smacks of dusty old classrooms and the droning of boring and repetitive lessons and consequently, it is ineffective.

"The Mystery of Nils" is different because your main focus is to just read and enjoy the story!

And that's why it works.

You concentrate on reading and understanding the story. The *formal study* happens another way!

This is a process known as *guided discovery*.

So what is guided discovery?

Well, rather than teaching you a particular grammar rule in an abstract way, you first see the grammar rule being used in the story itself - in context - so you get to learn how it works in a natural way.

This means the course syllabus emerges from the story. (Doesn't that sound more exciting than *normal* textbooks?) You discover the rules by yourself (with help from the story), which makes learning much more effective.

This means you get to enjoy learning Norwegian first and foremost rather than get bogged down in technicalities from the start. It's a fun way to begin your Norwegian learning experience.

Self-study and online learning are the most flexible ways to learn anything as you can base your learning around your lifestyle rather than working to the schedule of a rigid language school. By being able to work on your Norwegian in your lunch break, on your commute, in a cafe, or at home, you have the flexibility to learn at your speed, making it much easier to be successful.

CHAPTER THREE

PRACTICING NORWEGIAN ON YOUR OWN

It is very important to regularly practice the Norwegian you have learned even if it is just talking out loud to yourself. To really succeed in Norwegian (become fluent), it is essential to practice with a native speaker, but until you have found someone to practice with, here are some ways to practice by yourself.

Think in Norwegian

One of the main things about learning to speak a language is that you always have to learn to think in the language.

If you're always thinking in English when you speak Norwegian, you need to translate everything in your head while you speak. That's not easy and takes time.

It doesn't matter how fluent your Norwegian is; it's always hard to switch between two languages in your mind.

That's why you need to start thinking in Norwegian as well as speaking it. You can do this during your daily life.

If you discover a new word in Norwegian, reach for your Norwegian dictionary rather than your Norwegian-to-English dictionary. (Don't have dictionaries?—Buy some. You will need them; they can be your best friends while learning Norwegian.)

Think out loud

Now that you're already thinking in Norwegian—why don't you think out loud?

Talking to yourself whenever you're on your own is a great way to improve your language-speaking skills.

When you're reading books in Norwegian, try doing it out loud, too.

The problem with speaking on your own is when you make mistakes. There's nobody there to correct you.

However, it's helpful to improve your ability to speak out loud, even if you make the occasional error.

Talk to the mirror

Stand in front of a mirror and talk in Norwegian.

You could pick a topic to talk about and time yourself.

Can you talk about soccer for two minutes? Can you explain what happened in the news today for three minutes?

While you're talking, you need to watch the movements of your mouth and body.

Don't allow yourself to stop. If you can't remember the particular word, then you need to express the same thing with different words.

After a couple of minutes, it's time to look up any words you didn't know. This will allow you to discover which words and topics you need to work to improve.

Fluency over grammar

The most important thing when speaking isn't grammar; **it's fluency.**

You don't want to be stopping and starting all the time. You need to be able to have free-flowing conversations with native speakers.

Don't allow yourself to stop and stumble over phrases. A minor error here and there doesn't matter.

You need to make yourself understood rather than focus on everything being perfect.

Try some tunge twisters (tongue-twisters)

"Tunge twister" is the Norwegian word for tongue-twister. This includes words or phrases that are difficult to say at speed. Try out this Norwegian tongue-twister about a fisherman's son:

Du ska ikkje kalle Kalle for Kalle, selv om moren til Kalle kallar Kalle for Kalle, ska'kje du kalle Kalle for Kalle, for Kalle hetar egentlig Karl.

Translation: You're not supposed to call Kalle for Kalle, even though Kalle's mother calls Kalle for Kalle, aren't you supposed to call Kalle for Kalle, because Kalle's real name is Karl.

Åtte kopper upoppet popkorn.

Translation: 8 cups of unpopped popcorn.

Byens beste baker Bjørn Brun, baker bare brune brendte berlinerboller.

Translation: The city's best baker Bjørn Brun only bakes brown burnt berlin rolls.

Fisker'n Finn fiska fersk fisk forige fredag.

Translation: The fisherman Finn fished fresh fish last Friday.

Det var en gang en sebra som ikke kunne se bra.
Så gikk han til en sebra som kunne se bra.
Så lærte den sebraen som kunne se bra,
den sebraen som ikke kunne se bra å se bra!

Translation: There once was a zebra that couldn't see well. So he went to a zebra that could see well. Then the zebra that could see well taught the zebra that couldn't see well to see well!

Kristine kjøper kjøttkaker hos kjøpmannen i Kjellstad.

Translation: Kristine buys meat cakes at the storekeeper in Kjellstad.

Lille snille Pernille griller piller på Nilles grill, mens lille Ville triller Pernilles snille krokodille som spiller trekkspill.

Translation: Little nice Pernille grills pills on Nille's grill while little Ville rolls Pernille's nice crocodile that plays the accordion.

Nye børster børster bedre enn gamle børster børster.

Translation: New brushes brush better than old brushes brush.

Fem flate flyndrer på et flatt fat.

Translation: Five fat fishes on a fat plate.

Leika dåkkå dåkkå mæ dåkkå dåkkå då?

Translation: Are you playing with dolls, are you?

If you can master tongue-twisters in Norwegian, you'll find that you'll improve your overall ability to pronounce challenging words in Norwegian.

Listen and repeat over and over

Check out Norwegian-language TV shows or movies to improve your Norwegian (there is a chapter dedicated to this later on).

Listen carefully and, then pause and repeat. You can attempt to replicate the accent of the person on the screen.

If you need some help to understand the meaning, turn on subtitles for extra help. If you come across a word you don't recognize, you can look it up in your Norwegian dictionary.

Learn some Norwegian songs

If you want a really fun way to learn a language, you can learn the lyrics to your favorite songs.

You can start with children's song and work yourself up to the classics.
And if you want a greater challenge, check out the Norwegian rappers. If you can keep up the pace with some of these hip-hop artists, you're doing great!

Learn phrases and common sayings

Instead of concentrating on learning new words—why not try to learn phrases and common sayings? You can boost your vocabulary and learn how to arrange the words in a sentence like a native speaker.

You need to look out for how native speakers express stuff. You can learn a lot from listening to others.

Imagine different scenarios

Sometimes, you can imagine different scenarios in which you have to talk about different kinds of things.

For example, you can pretend to be in an interview for a job in a Norwegian-speaking country.

You can answer questions such as: "What are your biggest weaknesses?" and "Why do you want to work for us?"

When you have already prepared for such circumstances, you'll know what to say when the time comes.

Change the language on your devices

Consider changing your phone, computer, tablet, Facebook page, and anything else with a language option to Norwegian. This is an easy way to practice Norwegian since you'll see more of the vocabulary on a daily basis.

For example, every time you look at your phone, you'll see the date in Norwegian, reinforcing the days of the week and months of the year. Facebook will ask you if you would like to "legge til venn", teaching you the verb that means "to add" - "legg til".

Seeing a few of the same words over and over again will help the language feel more natural to you, and you'll find it becomes easier to incorporate them into everyday life with very little effort involved!

Research in Norwegian

How many times a day do you Google something that you're curious about? If you use Wikipedia a few times a week, go for the Norwegian version of the website first. Next time you need information about your favorite celebrity, look at their page in Norwegian and see how much you can understand before switching the language to English!

Pick up a Norwegian newspaper

You can read Norwegian newspapers online. I recommend VG Nett (https://www.vg.no/) but there are plenty of choices to suit your taste. The online version of this paper also gets a lot of hits each day. You can also download apps and read the news on your phone. You can read the articles out loud to practice Norwegian pronunciation in addition to reading skills. This is also a great way to stay informed about what is happening in Norway and the world, and helps if you get in a Norwegian conversation.

Play games in Norwegian

Once your phone is in Norwegian, many of your games will appear in Norwegian, too. Trivia games force you to be quick on your feet as you practice Norwegian, as many of them are timed. If that isn't for you, WordBrain offers an interesting vocabulary challenge in Norwegian! (See the chapter on apps).

Watch TV Shows and You Tube videos

Don't knock Norwegian soap operas until you try them! If you follow any British soaps, you will enjoy them. Netflix, Hulu, Amazon and Apple now offer shows and movies in Norwegian, some of which include English subtitles so you can check how much you understand. You can also watch your favorite movies with Norwegian subtitles.

Don't have Netflix, Hulu, Amazon or Apple? Try watching on YouTube or downloading straight from the Net. You can also check out free Norwegian lessons on YouTube in your spare time. This is a good way to judge the stage your Norwegian learning has reached. If you are a beginner, look for lessons that teach you how to say the letters and sounds of the Norwegian alphabet. It will help with your pronunciation. (See the chapter on best Norwegian TV shows).

Get Norwegian-language music for your daily commute

Why not practice Norwegian during your commute? Singing along to songs will help your pronunciation and help you begin to think in Norwegian (not a good idea if you use public transportation unless, of course, you have a superb singing voice). Try to learn the lyrics.

You can get music in any genre in Norwegian on YouTube, just like in English. I suggest the following for language learners: Lene Marlin, Marit Larsen, Sigvart Dagsland, Kurt Nilsen, Alexander Rybak, Morten Able, Kaja Gunnufsen, Venke Knutson and Erlend Bratland. You can hear most of these on the Spotify Channel.

Listen to podcasts in Norwegian

While you're sitting at your desk, driving in your car on your way to work, or cooking dinner at home, put on a podcast in Norwegian. It could be one aimed at teaching Norwegian or a Norwegian-language podcast on another topic.

For learning conversational Norwegian, try Coffee Break Norwegian, (https://radiolingua.com/category/oml-norwegian/), which focuses on conversations for traveling abroad, like how to order coffee! If you are a true beginner, Norwegianclass101 (https://www.norwegianclass101.com/) is another great one. They have all levels of Norwegian for any student!

Duolingo (https://www.duolingo.com/) has also just added a great new feature called "stories": fun, simple tales for learners with interactive translations and mini comprehension quizzes.

CHAPTER FOUR

A GUIDE FOR THE COMPLETE BEGINNER

If you are a complete beginner, you can consider using this book as a guide on *how* to learn and *what* to learn to enable you to speak Norwegian as painlessly as possible. This guide will hand over the keys to learning Norwegian for any and all potential learners, but in particular, it is for those who think they might face more trouble than most. It'll be more than enough to get you up and running.

These are the main subjects we will be covering as you begin to learn *how to learn* Norwegian. You will probably notice that I repeat the idea of motivation throughout this book. That is because it is important! It is one of the main reasons people fail to achieve their goal of speaking a new language and give up before they really get started:

- **Motivation:** Defining your overarching goal
- **Step by Step:** Setting achievable short-term goals

- **Getting There:** Efficient Norwegian learning resources for beginners
- **Fun:** Having fun as you learn
- **Ongoing Motivation:** Staying motivated as you learn

We will go over each of these subjects in more detail later, but for now, below is a brief overview.

Definition of Motivation: a reason or reasons for acting or behaving in a particular way.
Motivation is critical for learning a language. Good, motivating reasons for learning Norwegian include:

- "I want to understand people at Norwegian events."
- "I want to flirt with that cute Norwegian at work."
- "I want to read Knut Hamsun in the original."
- "I want to understand people at my local Norwegian delicatessen."
- "I want to enjoy Norwegian soap operas or TV series.."
- "I need Norwegian for work so that I can communicate with clients."
- "I want to be able to make myself understood when I'm on holiday in Norway."

These are all great reasons for learning Norwegian because they include **personal, compelling motivations** that'll keep you coming back when the going gets rough.

They also guide you to **specific, achievable goals** for study (more on this later), like focusing on reading or on the vocabulary used in conversations on the dance floor.

Here are a few bad—but rather common—reasons for studying Norwegian:

- "I want to tell people I speak Norwegian."
- "I want to have Norwegian on my CV."
- "I want to look smart."

Why are these bad?:

These are very likely not going to be truly motivating reasons when you can't seem to find time to open that workbook. They also don't give you any concrete desire to pay careful attention to, for example, a new tense that you've come across and how it might allow you to express yourself better.

If looking smart is your honest reason for wanting to learn a language, perhaps you could just lie and say you speak something like Quechua, which few people are going to be able to call you out on. (If you are interested, Quechua was the ancient language of the Incas and is still spoken in remote parts of South America).

Learning a language is a serious commitment

It is rarely possible to learn a language without a genuine motivation for some sort of authentic communication. That does not mean it should be painful or boring. Throughout this book, I will outline methods that make learning Norwegian fun and interesting. When you are interested in something and having fun you do not have to consciously **TRY,** and strangely, this is when you perform at your best. You are in the *zone,* as they say.

Step by Step: Setting achievable, short-term goals.

As in life, once you are clear about your overall motivation(s), these should then be translated into achievable, short-term goals.

You're not going to immediately get every joke passed around the pub and be able to respond in kind, but you should be able to more quickly arrive at goals like:

- "I'm going to place my favorite restaurant order in perfect Norwegian." We go over this in the chapter entitled "Navigating the restaurant."
- "I'm going to memorize *and use* three words of Norwegian slang." We go over this in the chapter entitled "Partying in Norwegian."

I cannot stress enough the importance of correct pronunciation, as this will form the basis of your learning experience. There are a lot of free online pronunciation guides, make the most of them. It is also a good idea, if you have the equipment to record yourself and compare it to the native speaker.

If you want to take it a step further, there are some very good audio books in Norwegian published by Languages Direct) https://www.languages-direct.com/shop-by-language/norwegian They have a whole load of books and audio books specifically designed to improve listening comprehension. The books are graded for difficulty so that you can assess your progress with each book.

Talk when you read or write in Norwegian. *Writing* itself is an important part of language learning so read out loud (paying careful attention to pronunciation) and write in Norwegian as much as you can. Just like when you took notes at school, writing serves to reinforce your learning.

- Watch movies with subtitles. Imitate some of the characters if you want.
- Listen to Norwegian music, learn the lyrics of your favorite songs, and sing along with them.
- Join a local Norwegian group. You'd be surprised how many there are and how helpful they can be for new language learners. This will give you a chance to practice your Norwegian with a native speaker in a friendly and helpful environment.

CHAPTER FIVE

FLUENCY

What is fluency? Every person has a different answer to that question. The term is imprecise, and it means a little less every time someone writes another book, article, or spam email with a title like "U can B fluent in 7 days!"

A lot of people are under the impression that to be fluent in another language means to speak it as well as, or almost as well as, your native language. These people define fluency as knowing a language *perfectly*—lexically, grammatically and even phonetically. If that is the case, then I very much doubt that there are that many fluent English speakers out there. By that, I mean that they know every aspect of English grammar and know every word in the English language.

I prefer to define it as "being able to speak and write quickly or easily in a given language." It comes from the Latin word *fluentum,* meaning "to flow."

There is also a difference between translating and interpreting, though they are often confused. The easiest way to remember the difference is that translating deals with the written word while interpreting deals with the spoken word. I suppose, to be pedantic, one should be fluent in both forms, but for most people, when they think of fluency, they mean the spoken word. Nobody has ever asked me to write them something in Spanish, for instance, but I am quite often asked to say something in Spanish, as though this somehow proves my fluency—which is a bit weird when you think about it as it is only people who have no knowledge of Spanish whatsoever who ask me that and I could say any old nonsense and they would believe it was Spanish.

The next question most people ask is: how long does it take to be fluent? It is different for every person. But let's use an example to make a baseline calculation. To estimate the time you'll need, you need to consider your fluency goals, the language(s) you already know, the language you're learning, and your daily time constraints.

One language is not any more difficult to learn than another; it just depends on how difficult it is for *you* to learn. For example, Japanese may be difficult to learn for many English speakers for the same reason that English is difficult for many Japanese speakers; there are very few words and grammar concepts that overlap, plus an entirely different alphabet. In contrast, an English speaker learning French has much less work to do. English vocabulary is 28% French and 28% Latin, so as soon as an English speaker learns French pronunciation, they already know thousands of words. If you want to check the approximate difficulty of learning a new language for an English speaker, you can check with the US Foreign Service Institute, which grades them by "class hours needed to learn."

CHAPTER SIX

FORGETTING

We struggle to reach any degree of fluency because there is so much to remember. The rulebook of the language game is too long. We go to classes that discuss the rulebook, and we run drills about one rule or another, but we never get to play the game (actually put our new found language to use). On the off chance that we ever reach the end of a rulebook, we've forgotten most of the beginning already. Moreover, we've ignored the *other* book (the vocabulary book), which is full of thousands upon thousands of words that are just as hard to remember as the rules.

Forgetting is the greatest foe, so we need a plan to defeat it. What's the classic Norwegian-language-learning success story? A guy moves to Norway, falls in love with a Norwegian girl, and spends every waking hour practicing the language until he is fluent within the year. This is the immersion experience, and it defeats forgetting with brute force. In large part, the proud, Norwegian-speaking hero is successful because he never had any time to forget. Every day, he swims in an ocean of Norwegian; how could he forget what he has learned?

Immersion is a wonderful experience, but if you have steady work, a dog, a family, or a bank account in need of refilling, you can't readily drop everything and devote *that* much of your life to learning a language. We need a more practical way to get the right information into our heads and prevent it from leaking out of our ears.

I'm going to show you how to stop forgetting so you can get to the actual game. The important thing to know is what to remember so that once you start playing the game, you're good at it. Along the way, you will rewire your ears to hear new sounds and rewire your tongue to master a new accent. You will investigate the makeup of words, how grammar assembles those words into thoughts, and how to make those thoughts come out of your mouth without needing to waste time translating. You'll learn to make the most of your limited time, investigating which words to learn first, how to use mnemonics to memorize abstract concepts faster, and how to improve your reading, writing, listening, and speaking skills as quickly and effectively as possible.

It is just as important to understand how to use these tools as it is to understand *why* they work. Language learning is one of the most intensely personal journeys you can ever undertake. You are going into your own mind and altering the way you think.

- Make memories more memorable.
- Maximize laziness.
- Don't review. Recall.
- Rewrite the past.

How to remember a Norwegian word forever

You can consider this part of the book to be a miniature mental time machine. It will take you back to the time when you learned as a child does.

Kids have amazing brains. They can pick up two languages in early childhood just as easily as they can learn one. Early childhood also seems to be the key period when musical training makes it much easier to acquire the skill known as perfect or absolute pitch. And that's not all: kids and teens can learn certain skills and abilities much more quickly than most adults. In a way, it makes sense that the young brain is so "plastic," or able to be molded. When we're young and learning how to navigate the world, we need to be able to acquire skills and knowledge fast.

As we age, we lose much of that plasticity. Our brains and personalities become more "set," and certain things are harder to learn or change.

As adults in the rapidly changing modern world, where the ability to learn a new skill is perhaps more essential than ever, it's easy to be jealous of how quickly kids can pick up on things.

How does one go from being a baby, whose linguistic skills end with smiling, burping, and biting, to being a fluent speaker whose English is marked by appropriate diction, golden grammar, and a killer accent?

Normal, everyday children do this in about 20 months.

This brings us back to the question: how do children learn a language? And what lessons can foreign-language learners get from these precious children?

So, we're going to trace a baby's journey from babbling newborn to kindergartner. Along the way, we'll note the milestones of language development

Pre-birth

We used to think that language learning began at the moment of birth. But scientists in Washington, Stockholm, and Helsinki discovered that fetuses are actually listening inside the womb.

They gave mothers a recording of made-up words to play during the final weeks of pregnancy. The babies heard the pseudo-words around 50—71 times while inside their mother's womb. After they were born, these babies were tested. By hooking them up to an EEG, scientists were able to see images of the babies' brains when the made-up words were played.

To their astonishment, the babies remembered and recognized the words that were presented when they were in the womb.

You know what this suggests, right?

It points to prenatal language learning.

It turns out, the first day of learning language isn't when one is born, but 30 weeks into the pregnancy when babies start to develop their hearing ability. So, be careful what you say around a pregnant woman, ok? Somebody's listening.

0—6 Months

Newborn babies are keen listeners in their environments. They particularly like to listen to the voice of their mother, and they quickly differentiate it from other voices. They also learn to recognize the sounds of her language from a foreign one.

Baby communication centers on expressing pain and pleasure. And if you listen very carefully, you'll notice that babies have different types of cries for different needs. A cry for milk is different from a cry for a new diaper—although a flustered first-time father might not hear any difference.

Around the fourth month, babies engage in "vocal play" and babble unintelligible sounds—including those that begin with the letters M, P, and B. (This is when mommy swears that she heard baby say, "Mama.")

6—12 Months.

This is the peek-a-boo stage.
Babies pay attention and smile when you call them by name.

They also start responding to "Hi!" and "Good morning."

At this stage, babies continue babbling and having fun with language. But this time, their unintelligible expressions have put on a certain kind of sophistication. They seem to be putting words together. You could've sworn she was telling you something.

It will actually be around this time when babies learn their first words ("no," "mama," "dada," and so on).

By the 12th month, you'll have that nagging feeling that she understands more than she lets on. And you will be right. Babies, although they can't speak much, recognize a lot. They begin to recognize keywords like "cup," "ball," "dog," and "car."

And on her first birthday, she'll definitely learn what the word "cake" means.

1—2 Years Old.

This is the "Where's-your-nose?" stage.

Babies learn to differentiate and point to the different parts of their bodies. They're also very receptive to queries like "Where's Daddy?" and requests like "Clap your hands" or "Give me the book."

As always, her comprehension goes ahead of her ability to speak. But in this stage, she'll be learning even more words. Her utterances will graduate into word pairs like "eat cake," "more play," and "no ball."

This is also the time when she loves hearing those sing-along songs and rhymes. And guess what? She'll never tire of these, so be prepared to listen to her favorite rhymes over and over and over again.

2—4 Years Old.

There will be a tremendous increase in learned words at this stage. She now seems to have a name for everything—from the cups she uses to her shoes and toys. She gains more nouns, verbs, and adjectives in her linguistic arsenal.

Her language structure becomes more and more complicated. Her sentences get longer, and her grammar mistakes get slowly weeded out. This time, she can express statements like "I'm hungry, Mommy" or "My friend gave me this."

She'll start to get really talkative and ask questions like, "Where are we going, Daddy?"

By this time, you'll begin to suspect that she's preparing to ask ever more difficult questions.

The child has learned the language and has become a native speaker.

So, what are the lessons we can take away from children as foreign-language learners?

We've just gone over how babies progress to acquire their first language.

Is there something in this process that adult language learners can emulate in their quest to learn foreign languages? Well, as it turns out, there is.

Understanding this early childhood learning process has major implications for adult language learners.

In this chapter, we're going to peek behind the curtain and look even deeper into how children learn languages to reap four vital lessons.

Each one of these lessons is an essential part of linguistic success.

1. The Centrality of Listening.

We learned in the previous section that listening comes very early in the language-acquisition process. Babies get a masterclass on the different tones, rhythms and sounds of a language even before they see the light of day.

Without listening, they'd have no building blocks from which to build their own repertoire of sounds.

Listening is so important for language acquisition that babies don't fully develop their language capabilities without the ability to hear. Thus, we have the deaf-mute pairing. How can one learn to speak when one can't even hear others or oneself doing it?

In addition, children who suffer hearing problems early in life experience delays in their expressive and receptive communication skills. Their vocabulary develops slower, and they often have difficulty understanding abstract words (e.g., extreme, eager, and pointless). Their sentences are also shorter and simpler.

In general, the greater the hearing loss, the poorer the children do in academic evaluations.

Listening is central to language.

It's the first language skill humans develop.

And yet, how many language programs pound on the issue of listening as a central skill, as opposed to grammar or vocabulary?

Listening is deceptive, isn't it? It seems like nothing's happening. It's too passive an activity, unlike speaking. When speaking, you actually hear what was learned. The benefits of listening are initially unheard (pun intended).

Contrary to common belief, listening can be an intensely active activity.

So, as a foreign-language learner, you need to devote time to actively listening to your target language. Don't just play those podcasts passively in the background. Actively engage in the material. If at all possible, don't multitask. Sit down and don't move—like a baby who hasn't learned how to walk.

Take every opportunity to listen to the language as spoken by native speakers. When you watch a movie or a language learning video, for example, don't just focus on the visual stimulation. Listen for the inflections, tones, and rhythms of words.

It may not look like much, but, yes, listening is that powerful.

2. The Primacy of Making Mistakes

Listening to a one-year-old talk is such a delight. They're so cute and innocent. Their initial statements betray a string of misappropriated vocabulary, fuzzy logic, and grammar violations.

When a 1-year-old points to a dog and says, "Meow," we find it so cute. When his older sister says, "I goed there today," we don't condemn the child. Instead, we correct her by gently saying, "No, Sally, not goed. Went!"

We aren't as kind to adults. We're even worse to ourselves.

Ever since we learned in school that making mistakes means lower test scores, we've dreaded making them. Mistakes? Bad. And we carry over this fear when we're learning a foreign language as adults.

That's why, unless we're 100% sure of its correctness, we don't want to blurt out a single sentence in our target language. First, we make sure that the words are in their proper order and that the verbs are in the proper tense and agree with the subject in number and gender.

Now, something tells me that a ten-month-old has no problems committing more mistakes in one sentence than she has words. In fact, she probably won't admit that there's something wrong—or ever know that something's wrong. She just goes on with her life and continues listening.

Why don't we follow this spirit of a child?

We already know that it works because the kid who once exclaimed, "My feets hurt," is now galloping towards a degree in sociology.

As a foreign-language learner, one of the things you need to make peace with is the fact that you're going to make mistakes. It comes with the territory, and you're going to have to accept that.

Make as many mistakes as you can. Make a fool out of yourself like a two-year-old and laugh along the way. Pay your dues. And if you're as diligent in correcting those mistakes as you are making them, soon enough you'll be on your way to fluency.

3. The Joy of Repetition

When your daughter is around 6-12 months old, playing peek-a-boo never gets old for her. She always registers genuine surprise every time you reveal yourself. And she'd laugh silly all day—all because of a very simple game.

And remember how, when your children were around one to two years old and they couldn't get enough of those sing-songy rhymes? They wanted you to keep pressing the "replay" button while watching their favorite cartoon musical on YouTube. You wondered when they would get sick of it.

But lo and behold, each time was like the first time. They weren't getting sick of it. In fact, it got more exciting for them.

Repetition. It's a vital element of learning. If there's one reason why babies learn so fast, it's because they learn stuff over and over—to the point of overlearning.

Adults never have the patience to overlearn a language lesson, to repeat the same lesson over and over without feeling bored to tears. Adults quickly interpret this as being "stuck". This lack of forward motion is promptly followed by the thought that time is being wasted. They think they should quickly press on to the next lesson—which they do, to the detriment of their learning.

We repeat a vocabulary word three times and expect it to stay with us for life—believing it will now be saved in our long-term memory. Quite unrealistic, isn't it?

In the prenatal experiment where made-up words were played to babies still in the womb, each word was heard by the baby at least 50 times. (Is it really a wonder, then, that the baby, when tested, recognized the words?)

Repetition is vital to learning. In fact, many apps take the concept further and introduce the idea of spaced repetition. SRS (spaced repetition software) can be an invaluable tool in your language learning toolkit. Try out Anki (https://apps.ankiweb.net/), FluentU (https://www.fluentu.com/), or SuperMemo (https://www.supermemo.com/en).

Unless you're a genius with an eidetic memory, repetition will be one of your most important allies in the quest for foreign-language mastery.

Repetition can take the form of replaying videos, rereading words, rewriting vocabulary, re-listening to podcasts, and re-doing games and exercises.

Keep on repeating until it becomes a habit. Because that's what a language ultimately is.

4. The Importance of Immersion

Immersion can actually push your brain to process information in the same way native speakers do.

And is there anything more immersive than a baby being born and experiencing the world by observation?

Think about what the baby is experiencing. She's like an Englishman suddenly being dropped in the middle of China without access to the internet.

Everything is new.
So, you use your innate abilities to make generalizations, read context, listen to native speakers, and imitate how they speak.

Everything is on the line. You've got to learn how to communicate fast; otherwise, you won't get to eat—even when you're sitting at a Chinese restaurant. It's a totally immersive experience where you're not learning a language just for kicks or for your resume. You're doing it for your very survival. (That takes care of the "motivation" part of your learning.)

There's nothing fake about a child learning a language. It's a totally immersive and authentic experience—all their early language lessons are learned in a meaningful social context. I have yet to meet a baby who learned his first language by enrolling in a class.

For the adult language learner, immersion can be experienced remotely. One way of achieving immersion is by getting exposed to as many language-learning videos as possible.

Another way is something we touched on earlier: **spaced repetition**.

Remember that time you crammed information for an exam?

(Don't worry, we've all been there.)

You, like many others, may have spent an all-nighter memorizing every page of your notes and trying desperately to make up for countless days you decided to hold off on studying.

While you may have performed well on the exam, think about how much you recalled a few weeks after the test date.

How much of that information did you remember?

If you're like most humans, the answer is probably not very much.

Cramming does not work, especially when learning a new language.

You can try, but unfortunately, you won't get very far if you try to learn the Norwegian subjunctive tense in one night. Now, you may wonder, "If I was able to recall information so well at the time of an exam, why has it dropped from my memory soon after?"

Well, there's science behind this! Research proves that cramming intense amounts of information into our brain in a short period is not an effective way for long-term learning.

British author H.E. Gorst mentioned in his book *The Course of Education* that cramming is what "produce[s] mediocrity". What he means is that cramming doesn't provide us with the ability to think critically and effectively apply our knowledge in creative ways.

Yet cramming is still becoming more and more popular among students of all ages.

If it's so ineffective, why do we cram?

Fingers point to improper time management as the number one cause. If we better prioritize our time, we can more efficiently learn new information. By cramming, we may absorb information that can be easily regurgitated the following day. But say goodbye to that information because it's going to disappear at an exponential rate as time goes on.

Cramming trades a strong memory now for a weak memory later. Unfortunately, we sometimes cling to short-term gratifications and fail to strive for long-term benefits. Before you banish all hope for your memory, there's an alternative method to learning that may give your brain the love it needs.

In psychology, there is a theory of memorization and learning called the "spacing effect". The spacing effect is the idea that we remember and learn items more effectively when they are studied a few times over a long span of time.

So, is frequent repetition the solution? Not quite.

Since cramming is out the window, you may think it's smarter to study material over and over again. It's crucial to note that while repetition is important, not all repetition is created equally. You'll want to space out the repetitions each time you study a set of information.

But determining how long to wait in between studying can also be a tricky matter. If you practice too soon, your brain will begin passively remembering information, which will not stick over time. If you practice too late, you will have forgotten the material and have to spend extra time relearning it. Add to this the complexity of individual learning and memorization patterns, and you have a recipe for guaranteed memory loss.

Thankfully, there is the aforementioned software available today to help us pinpoint the sweet spot of optimal learning. Just when our forgetfulness dips below a certain level, these programs jump in and keep our brains on track.

Spaced Repetition Software

Spaced repetition software (SRS) computer programs are modeled after a process similar to using flashcards. Users enter items to be memorized into the program, and they are then converted into electronic "decks" that appear on-screen in a one-by-one sequential pattern.

Usually, the user clicks one time to reveal the question or front of the generated card. A second click will reveal the answer or back of the flashcard. Upon seeing the answer, the user then indicates the difficulty of the card by telling the program how challenging it was.

Each following card's order of appearance is not random. In fact, SRS programs use algorithms to space out when each card will appear again on the screen. Cards given "easy" ratings will appear later than cards given "hard" ratings, thus allowing users to spend more time studying the cards that are more difficult. The tough ones will show up more often until they are mastered, giving you the chance to actively learn them more efficiently than with other learning styles.

Using Spaced Repetition for Language Learning

To put this into context, let's pretend you spend an evening studying a hundred Mandarin words you didn't know before. You continue studying until you've completely memorized the words. Let's say it takes you an hour to do this.

Immediately after reviewing these words, your memory of them will be quite high. However, over time, you will naturally begin forgetting the material you learned. And since it was your first time learning these words, your use-it-or-lose-it brain is more likely to ditch this new material at a faster pace. The new knowledge isn't yet considered important enough to be etched into your brain cells.

However, the second time you study the same words, it will take you less time to master the set than it did the first time. Perhaps this time it only takes you 30 minutes to memorize the hundred words. Congratulations! You've completed your first spaced repetition.

So, does this mean you'll have to keep repeating the information you want to learn for the rest of your life? Not exactly. While it does require long-term review to keep information fresh on our minds, the time spent on review becomes shorter and less frequent over time.

With each successive review, it will take you less and less time to fully recall the information. As you begin mastering a set of words, you'll find yourself whizzing through each card. Eventually, information will become so memorable that you know it by heart. This is when you know you're ready to move onto a new, more challenging deck.

Self-discipline Ultimately Trumps All

Remember, while these programs may have wonderful language-learning techniques, they won't be effective unless you have the self-discipline to use them on an ongoing basis. If you're still at a loss for where to begin with organizing your own flashcards, check out Olly Richards's "Make Words Stick", a guide for language learners just like you looking to get more out of their SRS.

Make it a habit to open up and use the software mentioned above. If you set aside some time every day to do your SRS studying, you'll see noticeable results sooner than you might imagine.

If, like me, you sometimes want to get away from the computer and get back to basics, you can make your own flashcards and use them manually. You can buy packets of blank cards at the post office or at any stationery suppliers. Write the English word on one side and the Norwegian word on the reverse. You can choose your own words, but here are some to get you started. If you want to know how to pronounce them (this is absolutely essential unless you are already acquainted with Norwegian pronunciation), head on over here: https://www.norwegianclass101.com/norwegian-word-lists/

uke *(n) fem*   week

år *(n) neut*	year
i dag	today
i morgen	tomorrow
i går	yesterday
kalendar *(n) masc*	calendar
sekund *(n) masc*	second
time *(n) masc*	hour
minutt *(n) neut*	minute
klokke	o'clock
kunne *(v)*	can
bruke *(v)*	use
gjøre	do
gå *(v)*	go
komme *(v)*	come
le *(v)*	laugh
lage *(v)*	make

se *(v)*	see
langt *(adj)*	far
liten *(adj)*	small
god *(adj)*	good
vakker *(adj)*	beautiful
stygg *(adj)*	ugly
vanskelig *(adj)*	difficult
enkel, enkelt *(adj)*	easy
dårlig (adj)	bad
nære (adv)	near
Hallo	Hello
God morgen	Good morning
God ettermiddag	Good afternoon
God kveld	Good evening
God natt	Good night
Hvordan går det med deg?	How are you?

Takk	Thank you!
Nei (inter)	No
Deilig! *(adj)*	Delicious!
Jeg heter...	I'm... (name)
Farvel	Goodbye
Ja	Yes
Mondag *(n) masc*	Monday
Tirstag *(n) masc*	Tuesday
Onsdag *(n) masc*	Wednesday
Torsdag *(n) masc*	Thursday
Freitag *(n) masc*	Friday
Lørdag *(n) masc*	Saturday
Søndag *(n) masc*	Sunday
mai *(n) masc*	May
januar *(n) masc*	January
februar *(n) masc*	February

mars *(n) masc*	March
april *(n) masc*	April
juni *(n) masc*	June
juli *(n) masc*	July
august *(n) masc*	August
september *(n) masc*	September
oktober *(n) masc*	October
november *(n) masc*	November
desember *(n) masc*	December
null	zero
en	one
to	two
tre	three
fire	four
fem	five
seks	six

syv	seven
åtte	eight
ni	nine
ti	ten
kaffee *(n) masc*	coffee
øl *(n) masc*	beer
te *(n) masc*	tea
vin *(n) masc*	wine
vann *(n) neut*	water
storfekjøtt *(n) neut*	beef
svinekjøtt *(n) neut*	pork
kylling *(n) fem*	chicken
lam *(n) neut*	lamb
fisk *(n) masc*	fish
fot *(n) masc*	foot
ben *(n) neut*	leg

hode *(n) neut*	head
arm *(n) masc*	arm
hånd *(n) fem*	hand
finger *(n) masc*	finger
kropp *(n) masc*	body
mage *(n) masc*	stomach
rygg *(n) masc*	back
brystkasse *(n) fem*	chest
sykepleier *(n) masc*	nurse
ansatt *(n) masc*	employee
politimann	police officer
kokk *(n) masc*	cook
ingeniør *(n) masc*	engineer
lege *(n) masc*	doctor
daglig leder *(n) masc*	manager
lærer *(n) masc*	teacher

programmerer *(n) masc* programmer

selger *(n) masc*   salesman
That should be enough to keep you going for a while.

We will be returning to childlike learning in Chapter Thirteen—"Learning Like a Child," as this lies at the heart of learning without mentally cramming.

Children are new to the learning process. They constantly see and experience things for the first time. They pause to listen to noises, try things over again until they master it, observe language until they can speak it, and ask if they don't know what something means. As we grow, we identify other ways to efficiently gather information. However, with this, we sometimes stop paying attention to the details in our everyday lives that can provide us with fresh insight and information. Consider these tips on how to rekindle this childlike process for obtaining knowledge.

Take Time to Observe

Start paying more attention to the things around you. Take time to appreciate the clouds in the sky. Pay attention to how your coworker's, partner's, child's day is going. Become aware of the people you are in line with at the checkout counter. Have a purpose in your observation, whether it's to better understand human nature, be more effective with your time, or gain an appreciation for others.

Go Exploring

Coming across things you have not seen or experienced before can help you appreciate things like a child would. Hike on a new trail, visit a place you've never been, or try a different route to work. Look at the things you see every day with a new eye. Consider how you would perceive them if it was the first time you'd ever noticed them.

Learn from Everyday Moments

Pause to think about the things you do every day. This can be a good practice if you feel you don't have much opportunity to learn new things or if you feel you are not progressing in your education. Assess what you have learned during your day. For instance, did a conversation not go as well as you planned? Evaluate what went well and what could have been different. Consider how you can avoid a similar situation in the future. Write down the knowledge you have gained in a journal and review it occasionally. See where you have made improvements and how you have grown from these experiences. Note: This also helps with motivation.

Model Other People's Good Qualities

Start paying attention to the good qualities in others. Make a list of these traits and determine how you can emulate them. Work on the qualities one by one until you master them.

Take Time to Read

If you are busy, which most people are, look for ways you can incorporate reading into your schedule. Note: Unless you do not mind having to use a dictionary every minute, read dual-language Norwegian books (the translation sits alongside the page you are reading). These are a brilliant learning tool and hugely enjoyable. You will extend your vocabulary marvelously without even noticing.

Listen to audio books in your car, read on the bus, take a couple minutes of your lunch break, or put a book next to your bed where you can read a couple pages before you go to sleep. Or, to start you off, here are some Norwegian/English parallel texts you can try online for free:

https://lingojump.com/collections/learn-norwegian/products/norwegian-easy-reader-2

Try different genres. Ask people what their favorite books are and read them—not only will you gain more knowledge from the books, but you will learn more about those around you by understanding the books they like. Study famous and influential people and events in history. Read both fiction and nonfiction. Do some research on the life of the author. Find out what world and local events were taking place at the time the book was written.

Talk to Others

Share with others the things you are discovering, whether it's something you read in the news or heard about in another conversation. By talking about what you are learning, you can better understand and retain the knowledge you gain. It can also help you discover fresh perspectives.

Be a Hands-on Person

Find a new creative outlet. Research how to prune rose bushes and practice on the ones in your yard. Follow instructions on how to cut tile and create a mosaic table. Take something apart to ascertain how it works. Enroll in a continuing education course on NorthOrion, such as photography, ceramics, yoga, or bowling.

However you decide to do it, incorporate learning into your everyday routine. Select those methods that come naturally to you. Be willing to look at gaining knowledge as a child does, unembarrassed and optimistically. You may find that you can gain the same enthusiasm.

Please understand that when I say you should "learn like a child," I am not telling you to suddenly revert to wearing diapers and gurgling. I am talking about using some of the intuitive language learning processes that we use as children.

Adults have some advantages, which we will examine, and children have different ones. We can learn to use both precisely because we are adults.

One thing that is for sure: we don't have the same amount of time as children, so we need to optimize the time we do have to make time for language learning. But we can also utilize the time we spend doing mundane tasks to our advantage—listening to Norwegian, for example.

The other thing you can't do is fully immerse yourself in the language (unless you are moving abroad, of course).

Your brain is nothing like a child's. The latter is a clean slate, and yours is like a graffiti-covered wall. So, when we want to learn a language, we have to clear our minds as much as possible. This is where mindfulness is so useful—more on that later.

Adults have a huge advantage insofar as first - and second - language acquisition are basically the same thing.

Adults are further advanced when it comes to cognitive development. What's more, they have already acquired their first language. It gives them the advantage of having pre-existing knowledge!

All these factors influence the cognitive structures in the brain and make the process of second-language acquisition fundamentally different from the ones occurring when you learn a mother tongue.

As an adult, you have the huge advantage over a child of being able to learn the most important grammar rules of a language when you want instead of having to acquire them slowly and through trial and error.

As I mentioned previously, adults have pre-existing language knowledge. Children have to learn the mechanics of their mother tongue, while, as adults, we have a more developed grasp of how language works. After all, almost all of us know what conjugations or adjectives are. What's more, adults are outstanding pattern-finding machines—it's much easier for us to deduce and apply language rules!

To sum up—as adults, we can learn really fast. But it all depends on how much we want to learn. **Motivation is key.**

Learning requires effort. We know that instinctively, and it sometimes seems that there is no way around it. The trick is to make that effort enjoyable; then it will no longer seem like an effort. It is just like someone who is happy with their job compared to someone who hates it. One will wake up in the morning looking forward to going to work, and the day will fly by; the other will dread getting up and drag themselves to work, and the day will also drag on interminably.

Your language learning experience is up to you, and as an adult, you have the ability to make it as enjoyable and as challenging as you wish. It is a mindset. Once you learn to **see** your mindset, you can start to **choose** your mindset. As with everything—you will reap what you sow.

CHAPTER SEVEN

NORWEGIAN GRAMMAR

Yes, I know, and I'm sorry, but you have to tackle it sometime if you want to master Norwegian. Remember, if you are not interested in learning grammar (I can't blame you, although it makes things a lot easier in the long run), you can simply skip this chapter. If you prefer, skip it for now and come back to it later or learn it in bits—doable chunks. I actually recommend skipping backwards and forwards as you will find it easier the more you learn the spoken language.

If grammar really does get you down and you find it a hard slog, see the next chapter, which is on motivation.

Norwegian grammar covers a lot of territory and I'm making a bit of an assumption that you're at least a bit familiar with English grammar because you're reading this in English. If it's your native language, you probably had some lessons about the difference between a noun and a pronoun even if it was years ago at school.

There is some good news though because many of Norwegian grammar elements are similar to English ones.

Norwegian Grammar

Grammar is often the most feared part of learning a new language. After all, grammar has all of those rules and it can be almost impossible to memorize them all. In fact, the reason that many people feel frustrated when they are learning a new language is due to all of the grammar rules. Instead of learning about all of the myriad Norwegian grammar rules in the beginning, it makes sense to learn only what you need to know to start learning the actual language. Once you have the basics down, you will find that learning and understanding all of the other grammar rules come more naturally.

Norwegian grammar is not as difficult as some other languages might be. Learning the basics happens very quickly for most people, and it can be that way for you as well. Before long, you will understand Norwegian grammar well enough to gain confidence when constructing your own sentences. The order of the words flows the same in the language as it does in English.

The Norwegian Alphabet:

Below is the Norwegian alphabet. Note that the last three letters in the table are vowels.

Æ – Pronounced like an elongated version of the 'a' in 'lap'

Ø – Pronounced like the 'u' in 'burn'

Å – Pronounced like 'ou' in 'four'

Y is always a vowel in Norwegian and sounds more like the *y* in 'typical' than in 'type'.

a (a)	j (jod)	s (ess)
b (beh)	k (kaw)	t (teh)
c (seh)	l (el)	u (oo)
d (deh)	m (em)	v (veh)
e (eh)	n (en)	w (dobbleveh)
f (ef)	o (o)	x (eks)
g (geh)	p (peh)	y (yew)
h (haw)	q (koo)	z (set)
i (ee)	r (air)	Æ (a) Ø (air) Å (aw)

Verbs in the Norwegian Language

You will find that the Norwegian verbs are going to behave very similarly to what you see in the English language. The verbs have a central meaning, which is time or tense. You already know this from English. There is a past, present, and future tense. To change the timeframe, you would change the verb to a different tense. A good example would be "I was pleased", "I am pleased", and "I will be pleased". These cover the past, present, and future. It is helpful to know when you are speaking as well as when you write Norwegian.

In Norwegian, gender is going to refer to a type of agreement between words rather than people. For example, dame is feminine and it means woman. The word Ku, or cow, is also feminine. Words in the language are going to have either a masculine or a feminine form. This happens in English, although it is not quite as common.

Plural

Just like in English, you will have plural forms of words, and you have to make the number agree in sentences in order for them to make sense. You will find that in Norwegian grammar, you will not have to worry about gender when you make a noun plural.

As with any language, learning the grammar and intricacies is going to take time. However, Norwegian is not too difficult to learn.

General information about conjugating Norwegian verbs

First of all, Norwegian verbs are *not* conjugated in person and number (as they are in English). What does this mean? Let's look at some examples to illustrate the English conjugation of a verb versus the Norwegian conjugation of the same verb:

English	Norwegian
I **am**	Jeg **er**
You **are**	Du **er**
He/she **is**	Han/hun **er**
We **are**	Vi **er**
You **are**	Dere **er**
They **are**	De **er**

As you can see, the Norwegian conjugation of verbs is not affected by which person it is or if it's singular or plural, considering the correct form is *er* in all the different persons above.

Secondly, Norwegian verbs come in several different tense forms as in all languages. Let's look at the five most common and useful tense forms:

English	Norwegian
Infinitive	Infinitiv
Present	Presens
Preterite	Preteritum
Present perfect	Presens perfektum
Present future	Presens futurum

But before we start on that, let's go through how to conjugate Norwegian verbs that are regular and irregular.

How to conjugate regular Norwegian verbs

Regular verbs, also called *weak verbs*, are verbs that follow a standard pattern when it comes to conjugation. It is unfortunately no way to know whether a Norwegian verb is regular or irregular just by looking at it—this is something you just have to learn for each verb. A tip is to use the language and expose yourself to the language as often as possible. The conjugation of the most common verbs will then, after a while, come naturally.

Regular Norwegian verbs are divided into four categories. We will now look at the conjugation of one verb from each category. Remember that when we're talking about the *verb stem* or the *stem of the verb*, we're most often talking about the infinitive minus -e. The stem simply means the base of the verb – the verb without any suffixes (endings).

Category #1:

Form of verb	English	Norwegian
Infinitive	To throw	Å kaste
Present	I throw	Jeg kaster
Preterite	I threw	Jeg kastet/kasta
Present pefect	I have thrown	Jeg har kastet/kasta

Rule: when the stem of the Norwegian verb ends with more than one consonant (in our case: two consonants—*st*), the preterite form and present perfect form is often the stem plus *et/a* (more information about *et/a* is below under "How to conjugate Norwegian verbs in preterite"). Unfortunately there are exceptions.

Category #2:

Form of verb	English	Norwegian
Infinitive	To read	Å lese
Present	I read	Jeg leser
Preterite	I read	Jeg leste
Present perfect	I have read	Jeg har lest

Rule: if the stem of the verb ends with one consonant (in the example above: *s*), the preterite form ends with—*te* and the present perfect form ends with—*t*.

Category #3:

Form of verb	English	Norwegian
Infinitive	To live	Å bo
Present	I live	Jeg bor
Preterite	I lived	Jeg bodde
Present perfect	I have lived	Jeg har bodd

Rule: if the infinitive of the verb ends with a stressed vowel, the preterite form usually ends with—*dde* and the present perfect usually ends with—*dd*. A stressed vowel means that it's a relative emphasis ('more force') on that vowel in the word. Unfortunately there are exceptions to this rule.

Category #4:

Form of verb	English	Norwegian
Present	I rent	Jeg leier
Preterite	I rented	Jeg leide
Present perfect	I have rented	Jeg har leid

Rule: if you have a verb whose stem ends with either 1) a diphthong, 2) the letter *v*, or 3) the letter *g*, the preterite form will be the stem plus—*de*, while the present perfect form will be the stem plus—*d*.

How to conjugate irregular Norwegian verbs

Norwegian irregular verbs are often irregular because of a vowel shift in the verb stem of verbs in preterite. The present perfect often ends in—*et* and can also have a different vowel. Irregular verbs and their conjugation is something you just have to memorize like in any other language. Here are some common irregular verbs in Norwegian:

Form of verb	English	Norwegian
Infinitive	To be	Å være
Present	I am	Jeg er
Preterite	I was	Jeg var
Present perfect	I have been	Jeg har vært

Form of verb	English	Norwegian
Infinitive	To do	Å gjøre
Present	I do	Jeg gjør
Preterite	I did	Jeg gjorde
Present perfect	I have done	Jeg har gjort

Form of verb	English	Norwegian
Infinitive	To write	Å skrive
Present	I write	Jeg skriver
Preterite	I wrote	Jeg skrev
Present perfect	I have written	Jeg har skrevet

How to conjugate Norwegian verbs in infinitive

Form of verb	Rule that often applies	Example

Infinitive	Stem + e	Snak**ke**

The infinitive form of an English verb is the form in which you can put the infinitive marker *to* in front of. Examples of this in English are: *to talk, to swim* and *to listen.* In Norwegian the infinitive marker is *å.* The same examples would be like this in Norwegian: *å snakke, å svømme* and *å høre/lytte.* This can be combined with other verbs in daily-life sentences. Let's look at some examples:

English	Norwegian
I love to read.	Jeg elsker å lese.
She ran back to give me my pencil	Hun løp tilbake for å gi meg meg blyanten min.

Verbs in infinitive are also used in combination with Norwegian auxiliary verbs. When you do this, you do not use the infinitive marker, *å*, in front of the verbs. Here are some examples:

English	Norwegian
I can read.	Jeg kan lese.
I am going to do it soon.	Jeg skal gjøre det snart.

How to conjugate Norwegian verbs in present

Form of verb	Rule that often applies	Example
Present	Stem + er	Snakk**er**

Present (*presens* in Norwegian) is the form of the verb you want to use if you for instance want to express that you are doing something right now. An example of that can be (the infinitives are marked in **bold**):

English	Norwegian
What are you doing? I am working.	Hva **gjør** du? Jeg **jobber**.

The example above means that you are working right now. You can also use the present tense to express something that's going to happen in the future. Here's an example of this:

English	Norwegian
Our friends will come for a visit next year.	Vennene våre **kommer** på besøk neste år.

How to conjugate Norwegian verbs in preterite

Form of verb	Rule that often applies	Example
Preterite	Stem + et/a	Snakk**et**

Preterite is a form of a verb you generally use if you want to express something that happened at a specific point of time in the past. Many Norwegian verbs have preterite and present perfect forms that are the stem of the verb plus either *et* or *a*. Which one you choose is a stylistic choice, but *et* is more formal than *a*. Here's an example of a Norwegian verb in preterite in a sentence:

English	Norwegian

| Yesterday I **jumped** on a trampoline. | I går **hoppet/hoppa** jeg på en trampoline. |

How to conjugate Norwegian verbs in present perfect

Form of verb	Rule that often applies	Example
Present perfect	Auxiliary verb + (stem + et/a)	Har snakk**et**

Present perfect is in Norwegian most often used when referring to something that happened in the past without talking about a definite past time. With the present perfect the past event has current relevance. Norwegian and English follow the same pattern here, considering that both use the auxiliary verb *å ha/to have* in order to express this verb form. An example of this can be:

English	Norwegian
I **have tested** many products.	Jeg **har testet** mange produkter.

How to conjugate Norwegian verbs in present future

Form of verb	Rule that often applies	Example
Present future	Auxiliary verb + infinitive	Skal snakke

When you want to express something that's going to happen in the future, you use the verb form *present future*. The common way to do this is to use an auxiliary verb in present plus the infinitive of the verb you're using. Note that the infinitive is used without the infinitive marker. The most common auxiliary verb to use in this form is *å skulle*.

English	Norwegian
I am going to be famous.	Jeg skal bli berømt.
We're going to leave now.	Vi skal dra nå.

Another common auxiliary verb is *å ville*. Here is an example:

English	Norwegian
I want to/will leave next week.	Jeg vil dra neste uke.

Notice the difference between between *Vi skal dra nå* and *Vi vil dra nå*. The first example means *We're going to leave now*, while the second example brings in a nuance of wishing to do something. Compare it to: *We want to leave now*.

Conclusion

You have now learned how to conjugate Norwegian verbs in many verb forms. We've looked at the pattern both regular and irregular Norwegian verbs follow, and then described the most common tense forms *infinitive, present, preterite, present perfect* and *present future* in the Norwegian language.

How to inflect Norwegian Nouns.

Norwegian Genders

This article shows you how to inflect Norwegian nouns. By this time you should have learned how to conjugate Norwegian verbs, so it's time to look at the inflection of Norwegian nouns. The inflection of nouns in the Norwegian language depends on which gender the noun is. There are three genders in the Norwegian language: masculine (hankjønn), feminine (hunkjønn) and neuter (intetkjønn). Let's look at an example from each of the genders to see how they're inflected.

How to inflect Norwegian nouns that are masculine

Indefinite (singular)	Definite (singular)	Indefinite (plural)	Definite (plural)
En hund	Hunden	Hunder	Hundene
A dog	The dog	Dogs	The dogs

This example illustrates the general rule when it comes to conjugating Norwegian nouns that are masculine. You simply add the correct suffix depending on which form the noun is in. The table below shows these different suffixes.

OVERVIEW	INDEFINITE FORM	DEFINITE FORM
SINGULAR	None	-en
PLURAL	-er	-ene

How to inflect Norwegian nouns that are feminine

Example: Ei jente – jenta – jenter – jentene (=*a girl* – *the girl* – *girls* – *the girls*)

The rule on how to inflect a Norwegian noun that is feminine, is as followed:

Indefinite form, singular: – (none)

Definite form, singular: -a

Indefinite form, plural: -er

Definite form, plural*: -ene*

OVERVIEW	INDEFINITE FORM	DEFINITE FORM
SINGULAR	None	-a
PLURAL	-er	-ene

Note that you can also use the masculine indefinite article instead of using the feminine indefinite article (*en* instead of *ei*). It's therefore correct to say for instance *ei jente* and *en jente*.

How to inflect Norwegian nouns that are neuter

Et hus – huset – hus – husene (= *a house* – *the house* – *houses* – *the houses*)

The way to inflect a Norwegian noun that is neuter, is like this:

Indefinite form, singular: – (none)

Definite form, singular: -et

Indefinite form, plural: – (none)

Definite form, plural: -ene

OVERVIEW	INDEFINITE FORM	DEFINITE FORM
SINGULAR	None	-et
PLURAL	None	-ene

Exceptions

Be aware of the fact that there are several exceptions when it comes to inflecting Norwegian nouns. In most instances the correct way is to inflect the noun according to its gender as described as above, but in order to master the Norwegian language you must learn the exceptions as well. On the positive side, the exceptions only have minor differences in inflection. Here are some examples of nouns that don't follow the patterns above (the differences from the regular inflection have been emphasized):

Masculine

En politiker – politikeren – politikere – politikerne (=*a politician – the politician – politicians – the politicians*).

Many irregular masculine nouns follow this rule, for instance:

—-> En jeger – jegeren – jegere – jegerne (= *a hunter – the hunter – hunters – the hunters*).

Feminine

En/ei bok – boken/boka – bøker – bøkene (= *a book – the book – books – the books*). There are many irregular nouns that follow this pattern with a shift of vowel in plural.

Other examples of feminine nouns that are inflected with a vowel shift are for instance:

—-> En/ei hånd – hånda – hender – hendene (= *a hand – the hand – hands – the hands*).

—-> En/ei strand – stranda – strender – strendene (= *a beach – the beach – beaches – the beaches*).

Neuter

Et tre – treet – trær – trærne (= *a tree – the tree – trees – the trees*).

As you can see, there can also be vowel shifts in Norwegian nouns that are neuter.

Conclusion

You have now learned that the inflection of Norwegian nouns depends on the gender of the noun. The nouns often follow a fixed pattern, but there are also several exceptions.

How to inflect Norwegian Adjectives

Introduction

Now you have learned how to inflect Norwegian nouns we will learn to inflect Norwegian adjectives.

Inflecting Norwegian adjectives in attributive form

Norwegian adjectives in attributive form (attributive form = e.g. *'a nice car')* vary in forms depending on whether the noun is in singular or plural, the gender of the noun and whether it's in indefinite or definite form. Let's look at some examples. Here's a masculine noun with an adjective in different forms:

En kul gitar – a cool guitar (indefinite, singular)

Den kule gitaren – the cool guitar (definite, singular)
Kule gitarer – cool guitars (indefinite, plural)

De kule gitarene – the cool guitars (definite, plural)

The pattern for adjective inflection is identical for feminine and masculine nouns, but it's a bit different for neuter nouns. Let's look at an example:

Et fint hus – a nice house (indefinite, singular)

Det fine huset – the nice house (definite, singular)

Fine hus – nice houses (indefinite, plural)

De fine husene – the nice houses (definite, plural)

The examples above illustrate in a good way the different forms Norwegian adjectives take in attributive form. This can generalized be written with just the suffixes (the ending of each form) like this:

Masculine and feminine:

Singular: – and -e (indefinite and definite)
Plural: -e and -e (indefinite and definite)

Neuter:

Singular: -t and -e (indefinite and definite)
Plural: -e and -e (indefinite and definite)

How to inflect Norwegian adjectives in predicative form

There is also something else we have to address in this article, and that is adjectives in predicative form. This simply means that you for instance say: *the car is cool*, instead of *the cool car.* Another example of adjectives in predicative form is: *the house can be scary*. The inflection in masculine and feminine form is also here identical. Let's look at an example with a feminine noun:

Ei/en lampe kan være fin – a lamp can be pretty (indefinite, singular)

Lampa kan være fin – the lamp can be pretty (definitive, singular)

Lamper kan være fine – lamps can be pretty (indefinitive, plural)

Lampene kan være fine – the lamps can be pretty (definitive, plural)

Let's look at an example with a neuter noun:

Et fjell er ofte høyt – a mountain is often high (indefinite, singular)

Fjellet er høyt – the mountain is high (definite, singular)

Fjell er ofte høye – mountains are often high (indefinite, plural)

Fjellene er høye – the mountains are high (definite, plural)

Here's the conclusion on how to inflect adjectives in the predicative form:

Masculine and feminine:
Singular: – and – (indefinite and definite)
Plural: -e and -e (indefinite and definite)

Conclusion

You have now learned to inflect Norwegian adjectives in attributive and predicative form. We have touched upon definite and indefinite articles, but let's take a closer look at Norwegian definite and indefinite articles.

Indefinite and Definitive Articles in Norwegian

Introduction

In this part of learning Norwegian grammar we will tackle indefinite and definite articles. After reading through this you will know what the difference is between indefinite and definite articles, the most common Norwegian articles (or determiners), and how to use them correctly when speaking or writing Norwegian.

What are indefinite and definite articles?

Before we discuss Norwegian articles and their usage, it's important that we understand what indefinite and definite articles are and what the difference between them is. An indefinite article is in English *a* or *an* and it's used when referring to a noun that is non-specific, and not known from the context. We can for instance have *a football*. This football isn't a specific or known football – it's just a football.

The definite article is in English *the* and is used when you refer to something specific and known that has been mentioned earlier. You can for instance say *the football* if you talk about a specific and known football – not just any football. In short, the indefinite introduces the referent into the context, while the definite refers to an entity that is already known.

Indefinite articles in Norwegian

So, now we know the meaning of indefinite and definite articles. Let's look at Norwegian articles (=determiners) and see some examples of how you can use them. The most common articles in the Norwegian language is *en, ei* and *et* which you place before nouns according to their gender (note that for feminine Norwegian nouns you can choose to use *ei* or *en*). These are all examples of indefinite articles in Norwegian and are the equivalents of the English *a* or *an*. Here are some examples of how they can be used in Norwegian sentences:

Example 1: *I bought a new bicycle because the old one I had was so bad – Jeg kjøpte* **en** *ny sykkel fordi den gamle jeg hadde var så dårlig.*

Example 2: *I got this watch from a girl I know – Jeg fikk denne klokka av* **ei** *jente jeg kjenner.*

Example 3: *It costs a lot of money to buy a nice house – Det koster veldig mye penger å kjøpe* **et** *fint hus.*

As you can see, the indefinite articles in Norwegian and in English are quite similar – both languages have articles put before the noun in singular.

Definite articles in Norwegian

On the other hand we have definite articles. In contrast to the English definite article, Norwegian does not have a definite article to put before the noun (in English: *the*), to express that something is in definite form. Norwegian uses on the other hand the suffix (ending) of the noun to express this form. Let's compare two identical examples in English and Norwegian:

Example 4: The *house was very nice – Hus*et *var veldig fint.*

Example 5: The *car was driving past us – Bil*en *kjørte forbi oss.*

Example 6: *Have you closed* **the** *door? – Har du lukket dør*a?

The reason for the different endings in the nouns above is that the Norwegian nouns have to be inflected according to its gender.

It isn't always the inflection of the nouns you use to express that something is in definite form though. A very common definite article, called a demonstrative, in Norwegian is the word *det/den* (depends on the gender of the noun – you use *det* in front neuter nouns and *den* in front of masculine and feminine nouns). *Det/den* is the same as *that* in English. Let's look at an example where you use *det* as a demonstrative in Norwegian:

Example 7: That *house was very nice –* **Det** *huset var veldig fint.*

There are several interesting things to note about the example above. Firstly, it's relevant to quickly explain the difference in meaning between saying *Huset var veldig fint* and *Det huset var veldig fint.* When you use *det* instead of just the suffix (*-et* in this case), you say *that house* instead of *the house.* It's evident that when you're using *det,* it becomes more clear that you think *that house* was very nice and not another house. Therefore it is called a demonstrative article (determiner).

Secondly, *example 7* also illustrates an interesting aspect with the Norwegian language if you add an adjective in front of *huset* (for instance: *det* **store** *huset var veldig fint*). In English you can say *the red house* and you might therefore think that you can say *røde huset* in Norwegian. This is however not the case. The fact is that when you refer to a noun in definite form with an attributive adjective in front of it, you have to use the demonstrative *det/den* in Norwegian. Here are two examples of this:

Example 8: *The happy boy – Den glade gutten.*

Example 9: *The high tree – Det høye treet.*

Also keep also in mind that in the Norwegian spoken (norsk talemål) and written language, it's common to use the so-called double determination, *dobbel bestemmelse*. Both *example 7, example 8* and *example 9* are examples that illustrate this phenomenon. The double determination, *dobbel bestemmelse,* means that you have a demonstrative article and an adjective in front of a noun with a suffix attached to it in definite form.

It is however also permitted to write *den glade gutt* and *det høye tre* (you write with *enkel bestemmelse* instead of *dobbel bestemmelse*) if you're writing in bokmål (not very common though). This marks a difference between bokmål and nynorsk, considering that simple determination, *enkel bestemmese,* isn't allowed in nynorsk.

Note however that *den glade gutten* with double determination is also the most common expression in bokmål.

Conclusion

In this part of learning Norwegian grammar you have learned what indefinite and definite articles are and how they determine the nouns. You have got an insight into some of the most common articles in the Norwegian language and you've seen examples of the usage of these articles.

That's enough grammar for the time being if you are really interested in pursuing Norwegian grammar to an advanced level there are plenty of books and resources out there that will show you how, but as I've said from the beginning this book is about learning how to *speak* Norwegian and that is what we will continue concentrating on.

Strangely, learning Norwegian grammar will also help you with English grammar.

You don't need to know everything, though. If you're unsure about the difference between a subordinating conjunction and a coordinating conjunction, you'll probably be OK unless you're a teacher or a grammar textbook author, in other words you are a normal human being.

But at a minimum, it's best to brush up on these ideas:

- noun
- pronoun
- adjective
- verb
- preposition
- participle
- definite and indefinite articles

You should also familiarize yourself with the idea of an **auxiliary verb**, **conjugation** and the concept of **tenses**.

1. **Monitor your progress and be consistent**

This actually applies to many aspects of language learning, but it can be especially important for learning the nuts and bolts of a language.

If you want to learn something new, you'll have to dedicate time to it. The more time, the better, and the more consistent you are with that time, the better. But if you can only do 20 minutes a day, four days a week, that's still probably more effective than 90 minutes in one breakneck Norwegian-cramming session. Your brain needs time to absorb what you've learned.

At the same time, record new vocabulary, new questions and new thoughts in some way. If you like to listen to music or watch classic movies, (go to FluentU where they have classic Norwegian movies which are ideal for learning Norwegian) you may still learn well, but most people find that by writing down new vocabulary words, for example, they retain a lot more of the new vocabulary that they've been learning. It also lets them monitor how far they've come and identify areas for future learning.

CHAPTER EIGHT

MOTIVATION *(yawn)*

I don't know about you, but I usually need some pretty strong motivation just to get out of bed in the morning. Maybe, its age ... But I'm wandering off topic (onset of senility, no doubt). With me, it's usually the slow dawning of hunger and the yearning for caffeine, usually in tea form. If I can be bothered, I make it with (proper) loose tea in a teapot and pour it in to a bone china cup with a saucer. Why do I sometimes make it with a teabag in a mug and sometimes in a teapot and served in a china cup and saucer (a Royal Albert tea service if you must know).? Well, for one thing, it tastes a lot better when I make it with "proper" brewed tea and serve it in chinaware, but that really isn't the answer, as just dropping a teabag in a mug still produces a good cup of tea and saves a hell of a lot of time and messing about. The answer is really that when I can be bothered to make *real* tea it is usually tied in with that thing called "motivation".

I do have specific reasons for choosing to make real tea most mornings, which I will not bore you with. Some are practical and others are sentimental. The mornings when I don't make real tea also have their own fewer specific reasons, usually involving lack of time, or simply that I can't be bothered.

Sit back for a moment with pen and paper and list the reasons you would like to be able to speak Norwegian. Some reasons will spring readily to mind and will go at the top of your list, but others you might have to search a little deeper for and these are equally important. Have the list at hand, on a bedside table, perhaps, and give it a glance before going to sleep and upon awakening. The list may change after a while, but the reasons will be equally as important. They are your motivation, and you should reinforce them every day.

You don't have to use the same list all the time and writing it is just as important as reading it. Here is one that helps you to be positive about what you are doing. It is quite long as I have illustrated each point with an explanation, which you won't have to do as you will know what you mean. Feel free to take what you want from the list for your own use but don't forget to add your own. Only you know what really motivates you. I am indebted to Henrik Edberg from The Positivity Blog for the following list.

Get started and let the motivation catch up.

If you want to work in a consistent way every day, then sometimes you have to get going despite not feeling motivated. The funny thing I've discovered is that after I've worked for a while, things feel easier and easier, and the motivation catches up with me.

Start small if big leads to procrastination.

If a project or task feels too big and daunting, don't let that lead you into procrastination. Instead, break it down into small steps and then take just one of them to start moving forward.

Start tiny if a small step doesn't work.

If breaking it down and taking a small step still leads you to procrastinate, then go even smaller. Take just a tiny one-to-two minute step forward.

Reduce the daily distractions.

Shut the door to your office or where you are learning. Put your smart-phone on silent mode. If you are a serial web surfer use an extension for your browser like StayFocusd to keep yourself on track.

Get accountability from people in your life.

Tell your friends and family what you are doing. Ask one or more to regularly check up on you and your progress. By doing this, you'll be a lot less likely to weasel out of things or give up at the first obstacle.

Get motivation from people in your life.

Spend less time with negative people. Instead, spend more of the time you have now freed up with enthusiastic or motivated people and let their energy flow over to you.

Get motivation from people you don't know.

Don't limit yourself to just motivation you can get from the people closest to you. There is a ton of motivating books, podcasts, blogs, and success stories out there that you can tap into to up or renew your motivation.

Play music that gives you energy.

One of the simplest things to do when you are low in energy or motivation is to play music that is upbeat and/or inspires in some way. In the case of learning Norwegian, play some Norwegian music that have lyrics. There are also a lot of Norwegian-speaking radio stations online. I will come to those later, but for the moment, you can just run a search on Google and choose one that suits your tastes.

Find the optimism.

A positive and constructive way of looking at things can energize and recharge your motivation. So, when you're in what looks like a negative situation, ask yourself questions like, "What's one thing that's good about this?" and, "What's one hidden opportunity here?"

Be kind to yourself when you stumble.

Don't fall into the trap of beating yourself when you stumble or fail. You'll just feel worse and less motivated. Instead, try this the next time: be kind to yourself, nudge yourself back on the path you were on, and take one small step forward.

Be constructive about the failures.

When you stumble ask yourself, "What's one thing I can learn from this setback?" Then keep that lesson in mind and take action on it to improve what you do.

Compare yourself to yourself.

See how far you've come instead of deflating yourself and your motivation by comparing yourself to others who are so far ahead of you.

Compete in a friendly way.

If you have a friend also learning Norwegian make it a friendly competition to learn some task first. The element of competition tends to liven things up. You could also add a small prize for extra motivation and to spice things up.

Remind yourself why.

When you're feeling unmotivated it's easy to lose sight of why you're doing something, so take two minutes and write down your top three reasons for wanting to learn Norwegian. Put that note where you'll see it every day.

Remember what you're moving away from.

Motivate yourself to get going by looking at the negative impact of not learning another language. Imagine where you will be in a year if you continue to learn. Imagine where you will be in five years if you continue to learn. Don't throw it away by giving up.

Be grateful for what you've got.

To put your focus on what you still have and who you are, ask yourself a question like, "What are three things I sometimes take for granted but can be grateful for in my life?" One possible answer could be: "I have a roof over my head, clean water to drink, and food to eat.

Mix things up.

A rut will kill motivation, so mix things up. Make a competition out of a task with yourself

Declutter your workspace.

Take a couple of minutes to clean your workspace up. I find that having an uncluttered and minimalistic workspace helps me to think more clearly, and I feel more focused and ready to tackle the next task.

Reduce your to-do list to just one item.

An over-stuffed to-do list can be a real motivation killer, so reduce it to the one that's most important to you right now (hopefully, learning Norwegian), or the one you've been procrastinating doing. If you like, have another list with tasks to do later on and tuck it away somewhere where you can't see it.

Don't forget about the breaks.

If you are working from home try working for 45 minutes each hour and use the rest for a break where you eat a snack or get out for some fresh air. You'll get more done in a day and week and do work of higher quality because your energy, focus, and motivation will simply last longer.

Adjust your goal size.

If a big goal in your life feels overwhelming, set a smaller goal. And if a smaller goal doesn't seem inspiring, try to aim higher and make it a bigger goal and see how that affects your motivation.

Exercise.

Working out doesn't just affect your body. It releases inner tensions and stress and makes you more focused once again.

Take two minutes to look back at successes.

Close your eyes and let the memories of your biggest successes - no matter in what part of your life - wash over you. Let those most positive memories boost your motivation.

Celebrate successes (no matter the size).

If you're looking forward to a nice reward that you're giving yourself after you're done with a task, then your motivation tends to go up. So, dangle those carrots to keep your motivation up.

Do a bit of research before you get started.

Learning from people who have gone where you want to go and done what you want to do can help you to avoid pitfalls and give you a realistic time-table for success.

Take a two minute meditation break.

In the afternoons - or when needed - sit down with closed eyes and just focus 100% on your breathing for two minutes. This clears the mind and releases inner tensions.

Go out in nature.

Few things give as much energy and motivation to take on life as this does. Go out for a walk in the woods or by the sea. Just spend a moment with nature and, the fresh air and don't think about anything special.

What about learning a bit of Norwegian while just laying on the sofa?

Coffee Break Norwegian

This laid-back podcast does exactly what it says on the tin. The lively presenters give you very small snippets designed to feel "like going for a coffee with your friend who happens to speak Norwegian". The podcasts go through the basics at beginner level right through to advanced conversations and are perfect for listening to while snuggled up on the sofa with a cup of something delicious. The basic podcast version is free for all levels.

(https://radiolingua.com/category/oml-norwegian/)

CHAPTER NINE

BEST NORWEGIAN TV SHOWS

Have you ever thought about learning Norwegian by watching Norwegian-speaking TV shows?

Instead of sitting in a classroom memorizing irregular verbs, you could be learning Norwegian by sitting on the couch in your pajamas, munching popcorn.

But if it were really that easy, wouldn't everyone be speaking Norwegian by now?

And come to think of it, wouldn't you have already done it?

Watching Norwegian TV shows is a way of *adding* to your learning, but there are some pitfalls to watch out for. And you need strategies to make sure that you learn as much Norwegian as possible while you watch.

In this chapter, we will look at the best Norwegian TV shows on Netflix, Amazon Prime and Apple (if you do not have access to these platforms, you can use YouTube). There is one important thing to bear in mind though, they are rare, so look out for them and prize them when you find them—they are treasures that will prove a great aid to your learning.

Learn how to make the most out of these Norwegian TV shows. This includes:

- How to choose the right series so you'll get addicted to Norwegian TV—and to learning Norwegian!
- What to do when you don't understand (a common problem that's easy to solve when you know how).
- More than just chilling out: study activities to boost your learning with Norwegian TV shows.

By watching Norwegian TV shows, you'll constantly be improving your listening skills. And if you use the subtitles in Norwegian, you'll also improve your reading and pick up vocabulary more easily. It'll even improve your speaking as you'll get used to hearing common phrases over and over, and they'll come to you more easily when you need them in conversation

Best of all, you'll be learning and enjoying yourself at the same time!

At this point, you might be thinking, "Sounds great, but I've already tried listening to Norwegian TV shows, and I didn't understand anything."

And even if you do understand bits and pieces, watching TV in a foreign language can feel overwhelming. Where should you start? How do you know if you're learning?

By the end of this chapter, you'll have all the answers.

A golden era of Norwegian TV

Norwegian TV has always been made primarily for a domestic audience. If there were any international aspirations, it was to near neighbors Denmark and Sweden. But the rise of streaming services combined with the unexpected worldwide success of Skam (more on that later!) changed everything.

All of a sudden, TV executives realized that shows filmed in a native language could break out after all. The popularity of Netflix has persuaded many people to try out foreign shows for the first time. The network has invested huge sums in producing original foreign shows, including in Norway.

Now, let's take a look at some of the most popular Norwegian TV shows available for you to watch right now. Some of these are on Netflix and others are on other services like YouTube. Also, lest you forget there is such a thing as Google!

Norwegian TV show: Norsemen (Vikingane)

Viking movies and TV shows are nothing new, yet very few of them are comedies. Introducing Norsemen! This is one of the few series ever (maybe the only one?) to have been filmed in two languages. Yes that's right, every single scene was shot twice, once in English and once in Norwegian.

The show itself? Well, the Guardian termed it as "Monty Python meets Game of Thrones" and that just about sums it up! Set in a Norwegian village in the early days of the Viking Era, Norsemen offers international audiences a rare glimpse of Norwegian dry humor.

Played by Kåre Conradi, the self-delusional Orm takes on the role of village chieftain while his brother Olav leads a raid. Hilarity ensues! While the show is charming, there is a fair amount of violence and gore packed into the six episodes. At the time of writing, Norsemen/Vikingane is available on Netflix.

Norwegian TV show: Ragnarok

Brand new to Netflix in 2018, Ragnarok had nothing in common with the Marvel movie, nor the Norwegian black metal band of the same name nor, in fact, to the third novel in my Ultima Thule series.

I'm sure most readers of this site will know that Ragnarok is an old Norse legend about the world's end. This show addresses that mythology, wrapped up in a high school drama with an environmental message.

If that sounds confusing, well, that's because it is. The show does indeed seem to leap around in focus a bit and the pacing of the six episodes is a little off. That being said, it's a fascinating concept and an entertaining show.

There are a few plot flaws, but that's the same with most fantasy shows. Aside from the fantasy elements, the characters are spot on and some of the best representation of "actual Norwegians" to be seen on the tele!

It holds the honor of being the first "Netflix original" made in the Norwegian language. The brains behind the show are Adam Price's SAM Productions, the creators of the Danish worldwide TV phenomenon Borgen.

Norwegian TV show: Beforeigners

The first Norwegian language production from HBO Europe is attracting critical acclaim from far and wide. "Time travel and murder combine in HBO's riveting Beforeigners series. It's a thoughtful, moving, often ribald and funny tale of worlds colliding," says Ars Technica.

The show's concept centers around "time migrants", people from the Stone Age, Viking Age and the 19th century who appear in modern-day Oslo. Yet it quickly morphs into a murder mystery. Two cops team up, one of which is the first officer with a time travel background.

One fan of the show is Lorelou who appeared on the very first episode of the Life in Norway podcast. She described Beforeigners as a "satire of western societies", offering up five reasons to watch:
"You get to listen to ancient forms of Norwegian language, observe interesting customs from the past, as well as Sami language and traditions, which are rarely (never?) on screen internationally," she says.

Norwegian TV show: Occupied (Okkupert)

While most of the shows on the list so far have just a handful of episodes, Occupied is for you if you want to truly binge. First aired in 2015 on Norway's TV2, Occupied is now more than three seasons old so there's plenty to get stuck into. Best of all, you don't need access to TV2! The series is available on Netflix in many international markets. But is it any good?

It's a political thriller with climate change at its centre. Set in the near-future, Norway's Green party sweeps to power following a catastrophic hurricane. They stop production of oil and gas in a bid to prevent any more climate-change disasters, but this causes Russia to stage an occupation. The curious twist? Russia has full support from the European Union.

Season one follows a series of characters including investigative journalist Thomas Eriksen and his family. Through their eyes, we follow the changes taking place in Norway, the political fallout and the rise of a Norwegian resistance group. We also meet Martin Djupvik from the Norwegian security service and Russian Ambassador Sidorova.

The brain behind the show's conception belongs to Norwegian crime writer extraordinaire Jo Nesbø, creator of the Harry Hole series. Vogue called the series "the most relevant thing on TV right now, a hyper-entertaining drama that treats the climate emergency with the seriousness it deserves."

So relevant is the series' premise that Russian authorities were none too pleased. The Russian Embassy even released a statement upon the show's release: "Although the creators of the TV series were at pains to stress that the plot is fictitious and allegedly has nothing to do with reality, the film shows quite specific countries, and Russia, unfortunately, was given the role of an aggressor."

Norwegian TV show: Bloodride

This one is definitely not for everyone. You'll likely know if it's for you based on this NME review: "Netflix's Norwegian horror anthology is 'Black Mirror' for technophiles."

The final two shows on this list are older, but no less interesting!

Norwegian TV show: Lilyhammer

The bizarre story of New York mobster Frank who ends up in Lillehammer on a witness protection program attracted almost one million viewers for its NRK1 season premiere in 2012. These days the full three seasons are available on Netflix in most global regions.

Not only did the Norwegian-American concept appeal, so did the casting of Steven Van Zandt, guitarist from Bruce Springsteen's E Street Band. His portrayal of big city American translated into small town Norwegian life is fascinating. It's sure to be of interest to anyone who thinks they might want to move to Norway!

Although the series was cancelled after three seasons, it ended on a high. The show dominated the comedy section at the Monte Carlo TV Festival, winning Golden Nymph award for best European series. Van Zandt also picked up the gong for best actor.

Lilyhammer also paved the way for much of what is great about Netflix today. It was the streaming service's first original production (they joined NRK early in the show's conception) and its success blending Norwegian and English pointed the way to the diverse stories, cultures and original language productions of today.

Norwegian TV show: Skam

Last but definitely not least, the Norwegian high-school sensation Skam. There were a lot of unique aspects to what would go on to become NRK's most successful ever production.

Skam's original release format was a series of small clips released throughout the week "as they happened." The clips were then pieced together and aired as a full TV at the end of each week. Each character also had real social media accounts, which allowed fans to follow along and interact based on those "real-time" snippets.

Each of the four seasons focused much of the story on the viewpoint of one character. The show wasn't afraid to tackle big issues ranging from mental illness and online bullying to the struggles of a Muslim girl balancing her traditions with the less restrictive Norwegian lifestyle.

Following the success of the NRK show and notably its worldwide fan base, the show was sold to many countries around the world. Now, several international remakes are out there. One Life in Norway writer tried to explain why he loved the series so much:

"What continues to amaze is the wide age range Skam draws. It seems to appeal to the young, middle-aged and the old alike, and Norway's original, at least, remains an accurate portrayal of the dramas, loves, relationships and friendships of teenagers in the 21st century, and this is perhaps the reason that Skam's popularity shows no signs of slowing anytime soon."

How to learn Norwegian by watching TV shows

So now you've got some great Norwegian TV shows to choose from. You can watch them as a beginner, but since they're aimed at native speakers, you'll probably enjoy them more if you're already at an intermediate level or above as you'll be able to understand more of what's being said and pick up new words without too much effort.

That said, it is possible to enjoy Norwegian TV at lower levels, too; you just need a slightly different approach. In this section, you'll learn how to improve your Norwegian by watching Norwegian TV shows at any level.

You'll learn:

- How to choose the right series to get you hooked on Norwegian TV shows (and, consequently learn Norwegian!)
- Study strategies to make sure you're learning lots of Norwegian while you watch.

Which series should you choose?

The most important thing is to choose a show you really like. It's pointless choosing a drama/thriller like *The Walking Dead* if you don't like this genre. You'll get bored and drop it in no time.

Try to think about the kind of series you get hooked on in your native language and look for something similar.

How do you choose the right show for your level?

Some shows might not be the best option depending on your level. Let's take a popular show in English as an example: *Game of Thrones*. Being an epic story, it is a pretty complicated and demanding series, especially for beginners and "older" vocabulary is often used: words like "jester" and "mummer" which are practically useless at this stage. The fact that each episode lasts about an hour also makes it difficult to follow.

The best way to find out whether a Norwegian TV show is suitable is by putting yourself to the test. Choose a show and play an episode with both the audio and Norwegian subtitles on. Watch the episode for a few minutes.

If you can follow the Norwegian TV show, great!

From now on, you will only watch this and other series with the Norwegian subtitles on, listening and reading at the same time. This will help you memorize and see the usage of words you already know, and it will especially, help you understand what's being said by getting your ears used to these sounds while you read the words. If you find words or phrases you don't know, you can pause the episode and write them down or add them into a flashcard app like Anki (https://apps.ankiweb.net). Over time, this will become more and more natural, and when you feel comfortable enough, you may even abandon the Norwegian subtitles.

If you found it was too hard to follow even with the subtitles on, don't worry; you still have some options.

You might struggle to keep up, either because

- There are too many words you don't know.
- They speak too fast.

If you are not already aware of it, there's an amazing Chrome extension that will help. It's called Language Learning with Netflix and has interactive subtitles that you can click on to get the definition in your native language. It also pauses automatically after every line to help you keep up. Give it a try—it could transform your Norwegian!

LEARN TO SPEAK NORWEGIAN · 137

Using a Norwegian TV show as a study resource

If you find Norwegian TV shows hard to follow even with the sub-titles on, then start with a learner series.

One of the reasons Norwegian TV series can be tricky to follow is that they're designed for native speakers—people who've spent their whole lives (at least 105,120 hours for an average 18-year-old) listening to Norwegian. No wonder they're tricky for learners!

Another option is to try using subtitles in your native language, just to get your ears more used to the new sounds.

One of the dangers with this technique is that you focus too much on reading the subtitles in your language and you don't benefit much from the Norwegian audio.

One thing you can do to get around this is to pay as much attention to the audio as you can. You'll notice that many words and expressions are repeated quite often by the actors.

When this happens and you don't know them, write them down in your study notebook or add them into a flashcards app like Anki (https://apps.ankiweb.net/). If you can't identify the words by ear, write down what's written in the English subtitles and use a dictionary to translate it or just Google it. Alternatively, you can flip to the Norwegian subtitles to see the expression written down.

In the meantime, keep studying Norwegian and learning more vocabulary, and over time, you'll notice that you understand more of the sentences without even reading the subtitles anymore. At this point, take the test above again to check if you can move onto the Norwegian subtitles phase.

Activities to boost your learning with Norwegian TV shows

Sometimes, when you're watching Norwegian TV shows, it feels magical. You're sitting there in your sweatpants, eating ice-cream and learning Norwegian at the same time. It's a win-win scenario.

But then a niggling doubt creeps in... Is this enough? Shouldn't I be doing more to learn Norwegian? While watching Norwegian TV can do a lot for your listening and speaking, there are more focused activities you can do to accelerate your learning.

The best bit—they still involve watching some TV!

The reality is that TV and films help you speak naturally and understand more.

If you spend all of your time just learning the slow and stilted dialogues that you find in textbooks, you'll probably end up speaking in a slow and stilted way.

Alternatively, if you listen to lots of realistic conversations in TV series and films, over time, you'll start speaking in a more natural way.

The same goes for understanding: if you only listen to learner materials, you'll get used to hearing a version of the language that's been watered down for foreigners. You might get a shock when you hear people using it in real life!

On the flip side, if you get used to hearing realistic dialogues in TV series and films (even if it's tricky at first!), you'll be much better equipped to follow conversations in the real world.

I'm not suggesting you try to learn a language entirely by watching TV and films. Learner materials like textbooks and audio courses have their place in a language learner's toolkit. And as previously stated, speaking practice is essential to perfecting Norwegian.

Foreign-language TV series and films are like handy supplements that can help you bridge the gap between learner materials and how people actually talk.

What if I don't understand anything?

When people think of learning a language by watching TV, they sometimes imagine learning through something akin to osmosis—the idea that if you listen to a stream of undecipherable syllables for long enough, it will eventually start to make some sort of sense.

But it doesn't work like that.

To learn, you first have to understand the language. Once you get to a high(ish) level where you can pick out a fair amount of what the characters are saying, you can learn a lot from just sitting back and listening.

What if you're not there yet?

Before that, if you want to learn a language by watching TV and films, it's important to do activities that'll help you understand the dialogues. The following activities will help you do just that.

How to learn a language by watching TV and films: what you'll need

First, you'll need a film, TV series, or YouTube video with two sets of subtitles: one in the language you're learning and one in your native language. This used to be tricky, but with YouTube, Netflix, Amazon and Apple it's getting easier and easier to find videos that are subtitled in multiple languages. Aim for videos where people speak in a modern and natural way (i.e., no period dramas).

One of the best of these is *Authentic Norwegian* on YouTube. The presenters interview people on the street, so you get used to hearing natives speak in a natural and spontaneous way. What's more, the videos are subtitled both in the target language and in English.

Another one is *Simple Norwegian,* it is particularly good as it has its own spin-off channels where they add fun and interesting videos a couple of times a week. If you're a beginner and you find these kinds of videos overwhelming (too many new words and grammar points), they also have a "super easy" series that you can use to get started.

Write what you hear

One super task to boost your listening skills is to use the videos as a dictation:

- Listen to very small pieces of the video (a few seconds each) and write down what you hear.
- Listen several times until you can't pick out any more.
- Compare what you wrote against the subtitles.
- Look up new words in a dictionary and write them down so you can review them later.

Often you'll see words and phrases that you understand on the page but couldn't pick out in the listening. You can now focus on the difference between how words are written and how people actually say them in real life.

This is your chance to become an expert at listening.

Make it your mission to become aware of these differences. Do speakers squash certain words together? Do they cut out some sounds or words completely? You may notice some things that native speakers have never realized about their own language and that teachers won't teach you.

Here is an example:

- In spoken English, "do you" often sounds like "dew," and want sounds like "one." So the phrase "do you want it" is pronounced like "dew one it."

No wonder listening is trickier than reading!

An awareness of these differences is your new secret weapon for understanding fast speech and developing a natural speaking style: the more you pay attention to these differences, the better you'll get at speaking and listening to the language as it's used in real life.

Translate it

Another invaluable task is to translate small passages into your native language and back into the language you're learning. After you've done this, you can check what you wrote in your target language against the original subtitles.

Ideally, you should translate the passage into your native language one day and back into your target language the day after so that you have to use your existing knowledge about grammar and vocabulary to recreate the dialogue (rather than just relying on memory).

This technique works because it gives you the chance to practice creating sentences in your target language and then compare them against the sentences of native speakers. In this way, you'll be able to see the gap between how you use the language and how the experts (the native speakers) do it. This will help you learn to express ideas and concepts like they do.

Comparing your performance to the experts' and taking steps to close the gap is a key element of deliberate practice, a powerful way to master new skills that is supported by decades of research.

Get into character.

One fun way to learn a language from TV and films is to learn a character's part from a short scene. Choose a character you like and pretend to be them. Learn their lines and mimic their pronunciation as closely as possible. You can even try to copy their body language. This is a great method for a couple of reasons:

- It's an entertaining way to memorize vocabulary and grammar structures.
- By pretending to be a native speaker, you start to feel like one – it's a fun way to immerse yourself in the culture.

If you are really up for it, record yourself and compare it to the original. Once you get over the cringe factor of seeing yourself on video or hearing your own voice, you'll be able to spot some differences between yourself and the original, which will give you valuable insight into the areas you need to improve. For example: does your "r" sound very different to theirs? Did you forget a word or grammar point?

Talk about it

A great way to improve your speaking skills is the key word method:

- As you watch a scene, write down key words or new vocabulary.
- Once you've finished watching, look at your list of words and use them as prompts to speak aloud for a few minutes about what you just saw.

As well as helping you practice your speaking skills, this method gives you the chance to use the new words you just learned, which will help you remember them more easily in the future.

Just relax and chill out

If you're feeling tired or overstretched and the previous four steps feel too much like hard work, you can use films and TV as a non-strenuous way to keep up your language learning routine. Get yourself a nice hot drink, make yourself comfortable on the sofa, put on a film or TV series and try to follow what's going on. Even if most of it washes over you, it's better than nothing.

While you obviously can't learn a language entirely by doing this, it's still handy because it helps you build the following four skills:

- Get used to trying to understand what's going on even if there's lots of ambiguity and you only understand the odd word (a useful skill to develop for real-life conversations!).
- Get your ears used to the intonation and sounds of the language.
- Become familiar with words and expressions that are repeated a lot.
- Stay in your language routine during times when you can't be bothered to study.

Don't underestimate the value of this last point: if you skip language learning completely during periods when you're tired or busy, you'll get out of the routine and probably end up feeling guilty. As time passes, it'll get harder and harder to get started again. But if you keep it up on those days, even by just watching a few minutes of something on the sofa, you'll stay in the routine and find it easy to put in more effort once you get your time and energy back.

CHAPTER TEN

NAVIGATING THE RESTAURANT

Who doesn't love to eat?

Explore delicious local foods while abroad—you won't be sorry! Or if you are very, very lucky, go to a Norwegian restaurant in your home town, (you are more likely to have success searching out general Scandinavian cuisine though!).

Spending time at restaurants or bars can really factor into your cultural immersion and Norwegian-language-learning experience.

Access to a fully equipped kitchen can be hard to come by while traveling, and you may well prefer to dedicate your time to seeing the sights rather than grocery shopping (though I'll be the first to tell you that exploring a local market can be extremely fun). Talk to locals, find out where the hot spots are, and ask about regional cuisine. People love to talk about food as much as they love to eat it!

No plans to travel? Join in on the fun by visiting a Norwegian or Scandinavian bar with Norwegian-speaking staff.

You may be worried about your pronunciation, especially if you are not familiar with phonetic spelling. Don't worry; there are a ton of resources online that can help you hear and speak Norwegian words. They are mentioned throughout the book and in the bibliography and at the end. Use them and practice out loud as much as possible.

Alternatively, sign up for my newsletter at my web site: https://stephenhernandez.co.uk/

Some classic Norwegian foods

Norwegian Food has many similarities with Swedish food and Danish food as well as Icelandic food, but Norwegian Cuisine also consists of some unique dishes and ways to prepare the food.

Traditional food in Norway can be eaten at restaurants throughout the country, and some places even prepare the dishes like the old recipes whereas some modern restaurants will prepare traditional Norwegian dishes with a modern touch.

Fårikål

Fårikål is a hearty stew which is quite easy to prepare, and a popular dish in the cold winter months. There is even a dedicated day of the year when you eat Fårikål.

It's commonly eaten in the western parts of Norway, but you can also find some good places to eat Fårikål in Oslo, such as Dovrehallen.

Surslid (Pickled Herring)

Pickled Herring or Sursild as its called in Norwegian is quite common and can be found in almost every supermarket. Pickled Herring is an integral part of Scandinavian cuisine as well as the Baltic countries and the Netherlands.

You could also eat herring prepared in other ways, such as fried herring.

Finnbiff

If you're traveling to the northern parts of Norway, you might get the chance to eat Finnbiff, which is another traditional food from Norway, made with sauteed reindeer meat, served with sauce in stew form.

It's also popular in the Lapland region of Sweden and Finland as well as Russia.

Kjøttkaker

Very similar to meatballs, and Kjøttkaker literally means meat cakes and is usually served with brown sauce, potatoes and carrots. It's a simple Norwegian dish, but very delicious.

It's best eaten homemade, but you can also find some gourmet versions in restaurants, and if you're lucky maybe you'll get invited for dinner hosted by a Norwegian person.

Smalahove (Sheep's head)

Of all traditional food from Norway, the Smalahove might be the most off-putting and weird Norwegian food to try.

This is not something that the ordinary Norwegian will eat on a weekday, but Smalahove is nonetheless a traditional dish which basically consists of sheep's head.

The sheep's head is either boiled or steamed for about 3 hours and is usually served with rutabaga and potatoes. It was typically a food for the poor people back in history, and sometimes the brain was cooked inside the skull as well before eaten with a spoon.

Brunost (Brown cheese)

The most popular type of brown cheese in Norway is the Gudbrandsdalsost. It's also known as Mysost and it's typically eaten on sandwiches or crispbread. It's made with whey and milk or cream.

Smoked Salmon

You can eat Salmon in many ways in Norway (just like Scotland), either cooked, fried or smoked. One of the most popular ways of preparing salmon is the one called Gravlaks, which is basically smoked salmon which has been marinated.

Salmon fillets are usually served with potatoes, vegetables, and some sauce.

Lutefisk

Lutefisk is another traditional food from Norway, which is typically eaten around Christmas. Lutefisk is made from lye and whitefish (normally cod) which has been dried and salted.

Sodd

If you want to try some traditional soups in Norway you should try Sodd (no sniggering please), which is a traditional mutton soup with potatoes and carrots. If you're visiting during the colder parts of the year, this hearty meal will definitely give you some welcomed warmth.

Whale Steak

For foreigners, this might be the most controversial food from Norway. Whaling isn't banned in Norway, and although a decline of the consumption of whale meats, many Norwegians eat whale from time to time.

It's not considered a controversial type of food in Norway. And you can find it in restaurants throughout the country as well as in fish markets.

Tørrfisk

Tørrfisk is a Norwegian delicacy, particularly around the islands of Vesterålen and Lofoten. It's a type of unsalted and cold air-dried fish, normally cod.

The tradition of Tørrfisk dates back to the 12th century and can also be cured through fermentation.

Lapskaus

Lapskaus is another Norwegian stew you can try. It can be made by fresh or leftover meats such as beef or lamb, but pork can also be used.

Potatoes are also included in the stew along with vegetables such as onions, carrots, rutabaga, celery root as well as various spices and herbs. There is a similar dish which is known as European sailor's stew, and the origins might come from the Vikings.

Pølse med Lompe (hotdog)

While regular hotdogs are sold and consumed in Norway, the Norwegian version with a sausage in potato pancake is more traditional and unique.

You will find Pølse med Lompe in kiosks, gas stations, IKEA, and around train stations, and it's a kind of Norwegian Street food.

Fiskeboller med hvit saus (Fish balls)

Fish balls in white sauce is another classic retro dish from Norway. It's easy to make and it's usually served with potatoes and carrots.

Norwegian Waffles

Belgian waffles might be famous worldwide, but Norwegian heart-formed waffles are just as delicious, usually served with jam and cream as well as a dash of raw sugar.

Lefse

Lefse is a type of Norwegian Flatbread made of potatoes, butter, flour, and cream. There are various types of lefse and you can roll various types of food in them.

The most common way to eat Lefse is to just add butter and rolling it up, but you can also add sweeter ingredients such as jams, lingonberries, sugar or cinnamon.

A bit more about Norwegian Food and Cuisine

Norway has a long history of fishing, and many villages supported themselves with seafood for many years. That holds true still today, although international food and other types of meat are commonly eaten as well.

Seafood remains an important part of Norwegian Cuisine, even more so than its Scandinavian counterparts. For example, Norwegian salmon and shrimps are world-renowned and exported worldwide. But of course, the highest quality is kept in Norway.

Sheep, lamb, and pork are other popular meats found in the cuisine of Norway. Many traditional dishes are accompanied by potatoes, carrots or some other root-crops and vegetables.

The sauce is also an important ingredient and the most common sauce is perhaps brown sauce, but there is a wide variety of Norwegian sauces that fit perfectly with the different kinds of meat and seafood.

Norwegian Meals

Norwegians usually eat three meals of the day, breakfast (frokost), dinner (middag) and supper (kveldsmad). Norwegians usually eat their dinner around 4-6 PM after work, and the supper usually consists of sandwiches around 7-8 PM.

Eating out

There is nothing drastically different about restaurants in Norway and restaurants in the United States, the UK, or elsewhere in northern Europe. But you will want to know how to say many of the same things that you would say in any other restaurant. For example:

Hvilken restaurant skal vi spise på? - Which restaurant are we going to eat at?

Hva slags mat serverer restauranten? - What kind of food does this restaurant serve?

Kan vi spise utendørs siden det er så fint ute? - Can we sit outside since it is so nice out?

Once you get to the restaurant, the **kelner** (server) will probably ask:

Hvor mange er dere? - How many are you?

And then he/she will probably say **følg meg** (follow me), bring you to your **bord** (table), and give you **menyer** (menus).

As you look through the **meny** you will see **forrett** (first course), **hovedrett** (main course), and **dessert** (dessert). You will also see **drikker,** including **alkohol, brus, kaffe, og vann** (alcohol, soda, coffee, and water), among other choices. When you have made up your mind, your **kelner** will ask something like, "**Er dere klare til å bestille?**" (Are you-pl. ready to order?). And you will say something to the effect of **"Jeg vil ha bakt fjellørret med poteter og erter"** (I will have baked mountain trout with potatoes and peas).

When your food arrives at your table, your **kelner** will undoubtedly say, **vær så god** (here you are) and you will say **takk.**

Mmmm...dette smaker veldig godt! - Mmmm...this tastes very good!

Jeg er mett. - I am full.

When you are ready, you will ask your **kelner** if you can have **regningen** (the bill).

Now you should be in good shape to eat out **på restaurant** in Norway.

Need help remembering some of these words? You can use an online resource like Norwegianclass101.com to hear them given context and cement them in your memory.

Norwegianclass101.com offers a growing collection of line-by-line audio, and more. It's an entertaining way to immerse yourself in Norwegian the way native speakers really use it while actively building your vocabulary.

CHAPTER ELEVEN

PARTYING

You're in Norway, and you've decided to sample the nightlife, here are some of the best places to go and what to expect.

Here are some things you should know before partying in Norway.

Norway is considered a cold country, but believe me when I say the nightlife there is nowhere near being cold or lazy. It is often electrifying, as you get to party hard with groovy music and high spirits, especially if you are in Oslo. There are concerts, DJ line ups, game bars and everything perfect to make your night a remarkable one.

When we speak of Norway nightlife, you must pick the destination wisely. Oslo, Bergen, Tromsø and Stavanger are among the places with happening nightlife in the country. This list features the best hotspots in Norway where you can make fun memories.

Kulturhuset, Oslo

Location: Youngs gate 6, 0181 Oslo, Norway

Some of the best clubs in Norway, Kulturhuset will greet you with generous space, good vibes and delicious food. Many facets of this hangout makes it a perfect fit for every kind of traveler. Other than a full-stacked bar, Kulturhuset boasts of spaces for library, public speaking and more. If you are visiting it late at night, make sure you go for prior booking as you will stumble upon long queues.

Stratos, Oslo

Location: Youngstorget 2, 0181 Oslo, Norway

One of the finest Norway nightclubs Oslo, Stratos will remind you of NYC in a way. This happening nightlife spot lets you enjoy mesmerizing views of Oslo as the bar is located on the eleventh floor. If you are here with a group of friends, the fun will only escalate and the night will become unforgettable.

The Villa, Oslo

Location: Møllergata 23-25, 0179 Oslo, Norway

Our Norway nightlife guide will be incomplete without mentioning this one for sure. This electrifying hub lights up the night with the lineup of talented DJs known for their groovy music. So, if you feel like dancing the night away, Villa has to be the place to be with your squad. It hosts amazing people, which means socializing will be fun too.

Lawo, Oslo

Location: Universitetsgata 26, 0162 Oslo, Norway

When the music is great and food is sumptuous, there is nothing more to wish for! Lawo is the paradise for youngsters looking for a taste of Norway nightlife. You will meet a bunch of well dressed people with high spirits on your visit to Lawo.

Blå, Oslo

Location: Brenneriveien 9c, 0182 Oslo, Norway

Where the night gets hypnotic, Blå will spoil you with its events, taking place frequently. This venue is a major pull for tourists and locals alike. There is something in the store always, whether you like concerts, shopping, drinks or football. The location is right beside a river, adding on to its beauty. Just stay updated with their upcoming events and plan your getaway accordingly.

Café Mono, Oslo

Location: Pløens Gate 4, 0181 Oslo, Norway

This is a bar and concert stage where you with your homies to chill! Cafe Mono present a variety of music genres, ranging from pop, country to jazz. Oftentimes there are new brands from different parts of the country. These underground artists are indeed amazing. There is a certain age limit, you must be above 20 years of age to enjoy this place. The food is brilliant too, and the crowd is decent.

No Stress, Bergen

Location: Hollendergaten 11, 5017 Bergen, Norway

Bergen, Norway nightlife is one of the most happening thing when it comes to nightlife in Norway. No Stress couldn't be named more aptly, after all it does a huge favor of eradicating all the stress in your mind. Everything here will make you forget about all the problems in your life. If you are looking for best clubs in Norway, this would be your pick, especially if you are a gamer at heart. After all, where else could you score a cocktail coupled with a game of Mario Kart!

Vaskeriet, Bergen

Location: Magnus Barfots gate 4, 5015 Bergen, Norway

With an array of cocktails, Vaskeriet is otherwise a quiet place for even a business outing, but the Silent Disco kicking off at 10 pm, turns the whole vibe around. Since this is a rather famous hotspot for a night out, you may stumble across a long queue as well, so make sure you time your entry well.

Bardus Bar, Tromsø

Location: Cora Sandels gate 4, 9008 Tromsø, Norway

The Bardus Bar in Tromso is inspired by the bistros in Southern Europe, and there is a blend of Norwegian culture in everything right from decor to the menu. Speaking of the menu, it is ever changing and can be seen as a gastronomical bible.

Bar Bache, Stavanger

Location: Øvre Holmegate 5, 4006 Stavanger, Norway

You cannot truly be in Stavanger without stepping foot at the Bar Bache. The drinks are moderately priced, and the nights here are worth cherishing. You can socialize or spend some lonesome time, enjoying a pint.

Okay, enough of the places, let's look more importantly at what you say when you want to get to one, are in one or, in some cases, the dreaded morning after...

Bar Talk

Drikkelag, Drikkefest
piss-up, booze up

Drikkekammerat
drinking buddy

Døddrukken
Blind drunk/rolling drunk

Drekka mer!
Drink more

Drikke opp
Skull, bottoms up (drink up)

Hjelp jeg har falt og jeg kan ikke rekker Øllen min
Help I've fallen and I can't reach my beer

Du har nok fått litt for
I think you've had one too many

Hva drikker du?
What are you drinking?

Jeg drikker for å forbedre mine sociale egenskaper
I drink to enhance my social skills

Vi hadde det skikkelig moro
We had some serious fun

Dagen derpå
The morning after, hangover

Alle disse pengene vil gå i dass
I'll piss all that cash away.

Ølbriller
Beer goggles

Tømmermenn
Hungover

Idioms and sayings:

Å være pling i bollen
Translation: To be a ping in the bowl.
Meaning: To be empty-headed/stupid (from the "ping"-like noise an empty bowl makes when you tap it).

Å få blod på tannen
Translation: To get blood on your tooth.
Meaning: To become inspired / driven to do something.

Å stå/sitter med skjegget i postkassa
Translation: To stand / sit with your beard in the post box.
Meaning: To have ended up in a stupid situation, that you may have cheated your way into.

Man skal ikke skue hunden på hårene
Translation: You shouldn't judge the dog on its hairs.
Meaning: You shouldn't judge a book by its cover.

Is i magen
Translation: Ice in one's stomach.
Meaning: Stay in control, play it cool.

Å gjøre kål på
Translation: To make cabbage of
Meaning: To finish something so that it is gone, for example by eating the leftovers 'gjøre kål på restene'.

Å være på bærtur / på viddene / ute og sykle
Translation: Berry-picking / on the moors / out cycling

Meaning: To describe someone who does not know what they're talking about or is lost (either literally or in a conversation).

Å være på pletten
Translation: To be on the spot.
Meaning: Where and when you're supposed to be.

Det er aldri så galt at det ikke er godt for noe!
Translation: It's never so bad that it's not good for something.
Meaning: The Norwegian version of "When God closes a door, he opens a window."

Å skrive noe bak øret
Translation: To write something behind the ear.
Meaning: To make a mental note of something; to make sure to remember something.

As with partying anywhere in the world it is best not to overdo it!

CHAPTER TWELVE

TRAVEL

You've bought your ticket, your bags are packed, and you can't wait to begin your journey to Norway.

Now, there is a simple thing you can do that can have a very big impact on your trip.

Learn some Norwegian travel phrases!

Your trip will be so much more fun and meaningful if you can communicate with locals.

Below are the bare essentials, the most common survival Norwegian travel phrases and words you will need on your trip.

Useful Norwegian travel phrases every traveler should learn

Before you move beyond greetings, here is a tip for learning the words and phrases in this chapter: the best way to study them is to hear them in use.

Norwegian greetings

Norwegian-speaking countries are generally very polite, and you must always be courteous and say, "Hello" and "How are you?"

Do not worry about making mistakes; most people will try their utmost to understand you and to make sure you understand them. Just try your best, and they will be happy to reciprocate. Some of the phrases you will be already familiar with from earlier on in this book but there is no harm in revision (or to put it more plainly repetition)!

Essential short phrases:

Greetings

English	Norwegian	Pronunciation
Hello	**Hei**	*hi*
Good morning	**God morgen**	*gooh mor-gehn*
Good afternoon	**Got ettermiddag**	*gooh eh-ter-mee-dahg*
Good night	**God natt**	*gooh naht*
Goodbye	**Hadet**	*hah-deh*
How are you?	**Hvordan går det?**	*vor-dahn gor deh*
I'm well, and you?	**Bra, med deg?**	*brah, meh dye*
Good, thanks	**Bra, takk**	*brah, tahk*

Essentials

English	Norwegian	Pronunciation
Please	Vær så snill	var soh snil
Thank you	Takk	tahk
You're welcome	Vær så god	var soh gooh
Yes	Ja	yah
No	Nei	ny
Excuse me (getting attention)	Unnskyld meg	een-shool my
Excuse me (when you didn't hear or understand)	Hæ? (like saying 'huh?', but not at all rude)	hah
I'm sorry	Unnskyld	een-shool
I don't understand	Jeg forstår ikke	yaiee for-storh ee-kah
Do you speak English	Snakker du engelsk?	snah-kerh doo en-gelsk

Questions

English	Norwegian	Pronunciation
How much is...?	Hvor mye koster..?	voor mee-eh koh ster
Where is...?	Hvor er...?	voor ehr
When?	Når...?	noor
Can I have...?	Kan jeg få...?	kahn yaiee fah

Eating out

English	Norwegian	Pronunciation
Beer	Øl	oul

Red wine / white wine	**Rødvin / Hvitvin**	*ruh-veen / veet-veen*
Water	**Vann**	*vahn*
I don't eat...	**Jeg spiser ikke**	*yaiee spee-sir ee-kah*
I'm a vegetarian	**Jeg er vegetarianer**	*yaiee ehr veh-geh-tah-ree-ah-ner*
Can we have the bill?	**Kan vi få regningen?**	*kahn vee fo rehh-ning-ehn*

Getting Around

English	Norwegian	Pronunciation
Left	**Venstre**	*hehn-streh*
Right	**Høyre**	*hoy-reh*
Straight ahead	**Rett fram**	*rett fram*
Turn left	**Ta til venstre**	*tah teel vehn-streh*
Turn right	**Ta til høyre**	*tah teel hoy-reh*
Bus stop	**Busstopp**	*boos stohp*
Train station	**Togstasjon**	*tog sta-shon*
Airport	**Flyplass**	*fleeh-plaas*
Entrance	**Inngang**	*een-gahn*
Exit	**Utgang**	*oot-gahn*

Numbers

English	Norwegian	Pronunciation
1	**En**	*en*
2	**To**	*tooh*

3	**Tre**	*treh*
4	**Fire**	*fee-reh*
5	**Fem**	*fehm*
6	**Seks**	*sex*
7	**Sju**	*shoo*
8	**Åtte**	*oh-tah*
9	**Ni**	*nee*
10	**Ti**	*tee*
20	**Tjue**	*shoo-teh*
30	**Tretti**	*treh-tee*
40	**Førti**	*fuhr-tee*
50	**Femti**	*fem-tee*
60	**Seksti**	*sex-tee*
70	**Søtti**	*suh-tee*
80	**Atti**	*oh-tee*
90	**Nitti**	*neh-tee*
100	**Hundre**	*huhn-dreh*

Days

English	**Norwegian**	*Pronunciation*
Monday	**Mandag**	*mahn-dahg*
Tuesday	**Tirsdag**	*teesh-dahg*
Wednesday	**Onsdag**	*ohns-dahg*
Thursday	**Torsdag**	*torsh-dahg*
Friday	**Fredag**	*freh-dahg*
Saturday	**Lørdag**	*luhr-dahg*
Sunday	**Søndag**	*sun-dahg*

Emergencies

English	Norwegian	Pronunciation
Help!	Hjelp!	yelp
I need a doctor	Jeg trenger lege	yaiee tren-ger leg-geh
I don't feel well	Jeg er dårlig	yaiee ehr door-lee
Call the police!	Ring politet!	reen poh-lee-tee-eht
Fire!	Brann!	brahnn

Why you should learn Norwegian travel phrases.

Even if you can't have a fluent conversation, native Norwegian speakers always appreciate when foreigners put the effort into learning a bit of their language. It shows respect and demonstrates that you truly want to reach out and connect with people while abroad.

You won't be totally reliant on your Norwegian phrasebook. Yes, your Lonely Planet Norwegian phrasebook has glossy pages and you love getting the chance to use it—but you want to be able to respond quickly when people speak to you, at a moment's notice. After learning the Norwegian travel phrases above, you'll only need your Norwegian phrasebook in a real pinch.

If you can express yourself with some basic Norwegian phrases, you are less likely to be taken advantage of by taxi drivers, souvenir shops and waiters!

The perception that all Norwegian speakers speak English is simply not true. Even in the big Norwegian cities you'll find loads of people that know very little English. You don't want to have to track down other English speakers every time you have a question or want to make a friend.

If you want to have an edge during your upcoming travels, take a moment to memorize Norwegian travel phrases. You won't regret it!

So there you have it: a collection of Norwegian expressions to help you get started on your new adventure!

Practice saying everything aloud so that you will remember some of the phrases without looking and learn how to say these phrases relatively quickly and smoothly. Just hearing them spoken aloud will also help in your comprehension when people are speaking to you

Take a small pocket dictionary with you. While you don't want to try to look up verb declensions in the middle of talking with someone, you can look up nouns quickly.

Better yet, take a phrasebook. There are tons of incredible phrasebooks (some that are partially travel guides), such as those offered by Lonely Planet, that are perfect for traveling and pulling out at a moment's notice. This way, if you ever forget one of your most important travel phrases, you'll be able to remind yourself

And if you find a regional Norwegian phrasebook that focuses on your travel destination, you'll find even more useful phrases that locals love to use.

CHAPTER THIRTEEN

LEARNING LIKE A CHILD

As promised in Chapter Six, we are going to revisit what it means to *learn like a child* in greater depth.

Why is it that when we look back to our childhood, it seems that we effortlessly learned the things we truly wanted to?

There are a number of factors that we can look at individually.

- To start with, there seems to be a misinformed idea that as young adults, we have less on our minds and that this makes learning something like another language that much easier.

Mindfulness. Before you turn away in disgust and throw this book to the other side of the room shouting, "I knew it! He was a hippy all along. Now he is going to get me to cross my legs and hum OM," I am not going to ask you to do any of those things. If that is your thing, though, please feel free to do it, although I will remain dubious as to whether it will help you master another language.

I know mindfulness is a bit of a buzzword nowadays. A lot of people have heard about it but are confused about what it really means. This is not a book about mindfulness, so I am just going to go over the basics. It means focusing your awareness on the present moment and noticing your physical and emotional sensations without judgment as you are doing whatever you happen to be doing.

The benefits of mindfulness are plentiful. It increases concentration, improves self-acceptance and self-esteem, strengthens resilience, and decreases stress. In a world where we are continually subject to stress mindfulness can provide an oasis of calm.

Mindfulness (being mindful of what you do), can also help you to learn a language much more easily because a part of mindfulness involves unconscious concentration. To achieve unconscious concentration as an adult we have to practice it, unfortunately, as it is a skill many of us have lost. It is not as difficult as it sounds, and in fact, it is quite fun. Just take time out, if you get a chance, and watch some young children at play.

Look at how hard children concentrate in whatever game they are playing. They aren't making a conscious effort to concentrate; they are concentrating naturally, thoroughly immersed in the game. This is mindfulness in its most natural form, and this is what thousands of people pay hundreds of bucks every year to achieve once again.

Now, see what happens if you get one of the poor kids to stop playing and ask them to do a mundane and pre-set task like taking out the trash. Watch the child's attitude change: she's now, not just annoyed and resentful that she has been taken away from her game, but the concentration that was there when she was playing has gone. You could say her mind's not on the job, and you would be quite right. The mindfulness has gone, but it will return almost instantaneously when she resumes playing and having fun.

Games, puzzles, and challenges are all fun to us when we are young and we devote all our mind's energy to them wholeheartedly, and that is what we will try to recapture as we learn Norwegian.

When you are actively concentrating on learning Norwegian, it is a good idea to turn off all distractions except the method you are using to learn. By this, I mean all the gadgets we are surrounded by, such as: the telephone, radio, Facebook, Twitter, Instagram - you get the picture.

Multitasking is one of those words that is bandied about a lot nowadays - the ability to perform lots of tasks at the same time. But in this particular case, multitasking is a bad thing, a very bad thing. It has been proven that it isn't actually healthy for us and we are more efficient when we focus on just one thing at a time.

Take some deep breaths and focus all your attention on your breath. You will find your mind wandering and thoughts will distract you, but don't try to think them through or control them. Bring your attention back to your breath. It takes practice, and like learning Norwegian, if you do it every day, you will get better at it. Also, learning to breathe better will bring more oxygen to your brain.

Before you start any learning, take a few moments to breathe and relax. If you want, do some light stretching. This allows for better blood flow before studying. Better blood flow means more oxygen to the brain - need I say more?

When it comes to studying, do the same as you did with your thoughts: if you make a mistake, do not judge yourself Instead, acknowledge it and move on. Be kind to yourself at all times. You are doing an awesome thing - be proud of it. Remember that old saying: you learn through your mistakes. It is fine to make mistakes; just remember to learn from them and not get annoyed with yourself.

Just like with being mindful, be aware of the progress you are making with your language learning, but also be patient and do not judge yourself or compare yourself with others.

If you feel like it, smile a bit (I don't mean grin like a madman) as studies have shown that smiling brings authentic feelings of well-being and reduces stress levels.

You will find your mind wandering. Everybody's mind wanders. This is fine and completely normal. Just sit back and look at the thought. Follow it but do not take part. Be an observer, as it were. You can label it if that makes it easier to dismiss, for example, "worrying," "planning," "judging," etc. It is up to you to either act upon that and become distracted or let it go and focus on the task at hand - learning Norwegian.

CHAPTER FOURTEEN

SPEAKING NORWEGIAN

Learning Norwegian vs. Speaking Norwegian

Why do you want to learn Norwegian?

This question was put to the students learning Spanish using an app called Verbalicity (https://verbalicity.com). This is what they said:

"My wife is from Mexico, and I want to talk to her parents who don't speak a word of English."

"I'm going to Guatemala next April, and I'd like to be able to have some basic conversations with the locals."

"We get a lot of Spanish-speaking patients at the clinic where I work, and I want to communicate with them better."

What did these people have in common? They all want to learn Spanish so they can use it in the real world. In other words, they wanted to **speak Spanish.**

Nobody ever wanted to learn Norwegian so they can stay in their house and watch Norwegian soap operas all day.

So, if the goal is to speak Norwegian, then why do the majority of beginners start learning Norwegian using methods that don't actually force them to speak?

This is the single biggest mistake that most people make when learning Spanish, German, French or Norwegian or any other language.

Most learning methods only teach you the "stuff" of Norwegian, like the grammar, vocabulary, listening, reading, etc. Very few of them actually teach you how to speak Norwegian.

Let's compare methods.

Methods that only teach you the "stuff" of Norwegian:

- Apps
- Audio courses
- Group classes
- Radio/podcasts
- Reading
- Software
- Textbooks
- TV/movies

Methods that teach you to speak Norwegian:

- Practicing with people you know
- Meetups
- Language exchanges
- Lessons with a Norwegian teacher online or in the real world

Many language experts, like Benny Lewis, have said that studying will never help you speak a language. The best way to learn Norwegian or any language involves more than just studying.

Let's say you are learning to drive for the first time. Your parents drop you off at the driving school for your theory class.

You spend many hours learning about traffic lights, left turns, parallel parking, and the dreaded roundabout. Your brain is filled with everything you'll ever need to know about driving a car.

Does this mean you can drive now?

No!

There's a reason why they don't give you your license right after you pass the theory test. It's because studying theory doesn't actually teach you how to drive.

You need to be behind the wheel, you need to get a "feel" for it with all of your senses, and you need to get used to making snap decisions.

Languages work in the same way.

To learn a language properly, you have to speak it.

Speaking: The one thing that makes everything else easier

You might be asking, "How am I supposed to speak if I don't learn vocabulary and grammar first?"

While it's true that a small foundation of vocabulary and grammar is necessary, the problem is that most beginners greatly overestimate how much they really need.

People spend thousands of dollars on courses and many months of self-study and still don't feel like they're "ready" to speak Norwegian. Speaking is something that they'll put off again and again.

Scientists from the NTL Institute discovered through their research that people remember:

90% of what they learn when they use it immediately.

50% of what they learn when engaged in a group discussion.

20% of what they learn from audio-visual sources.

10% of what they learn when they've learned from reading.

5% of what they learn from lectures.

This means that the best way to learn Norwegian is to start speaking from the beginning and try to use every new word and grammar concept in real conversations.

Speaking is the one skill that connects all the different elements of language learning. When you are speaking, you are actually improving every other aspect of the language simultaneously.

Speaking improves:

- Pronunciation
- Reading
- Writing
- Vocabulary
- Grammar
- Listening

Here's a breakdown of how speaking can improve your other language skills:

Vocabulary

Have you ever studied a word in Norwegian but then totally drawn a blank when you tried to use it in a conversation? Well, you will. Sorry.

This happens all the time because, although you can recognize the word when you see it or hear it, you can't naturally recall the word when you want to.

The only way for new words to truly become part of your vocabulary is to speak them repeatedly, putting them into real sentences that have real meaning. Eventually, the word will become a force of habit so that you can say it without even thinking.

Grammar

Let's say your friend asks you what you did yesterday, and you want to respond in Spanish:

What is "To walk" in Spanish?
"caminar"

Ok, time to use past tense, but should I use preterit or imperfect?
Preterit because you're talking about a single point in time.

What is the conjugation for "caminar" for the first person?
"caminé"

Your answer: "Ayer, caminé a la playa."

You may have studied all the grammar, but you would probably spend a good ten seconds thinking about this if you're not used to using grammar in conversations.

Speaking is the only thing that trains your brain and speeds up this thought process until you can respond in 1/10th of a second.

Listening

For many beginners, understanding native speakers is the number one challenge when learning Norwegian or any other language.

When you are having a conversation with someone, you are speaking and training your ears at the same time. You are listening "actively," which means you are listening with the intent to respond. This forces you into a higher state of concentration, as opposed to "passively" listening to Norwegian radio, for example, where you are simply taking in information.

Listening and speaking really go hand in hand.

Pronunciation

The first part of pronunciation is to understand how to correctly produce the sounds, which can be tricky, once you can do it right, the next part is about getting enough reps and saying the words out loud again and again.

Maybe at first, the words will make your tongue and lips feel strange, but over time, they will become part of your muscle memory until eventually it feels completely natural to say them.

Reading and writing

Norwegian word order is different from other Germanic languages, and much closer to English. Norwegian pronunciation is much easier for English-speakers as well. For example:

Norwegian letter(s)	English sound
d	silent at end of word; and in -ld, -nd, -rd
ig	ee
eg	ay
h	silent before consonants, such as in hv-
j, gj, hj	yuh, as in *yes*
kj, tj	sh, but softer and more palatalized (as in German)
sj, skj	sh
sl	shl
ki, ky, kei, køy	sh, but softer and more palatalized (as in German)
ski, sky, skei, skøy	sh
gi, gy, gei, gøy	yuh
g + other vowels	guh
sk + other vowels	sk
-egn, -egl, -øgn	g is silent
ng	nasalized, as in singer and not finger
æ	ah as in cat
ø	ay, but with lips rounded
å	aw as in saw

If you can say something in Norwegian, then you'll have no problem reading and writing it as well.

However, the opposite isn't true. If you focus on reading and writing, it will not enable you to speak better.

Why?

Because, when you're speaking, everything happens in **seconds**, whereas reading and writing happen in **minutes**. Only speaking will train your brain to think fast enough to keep up with conversations.

80/20 your Norwegian

Also called Pareto's principle, the 80/20 rule states that 80% of your results come from just 20% of your efforts.

This principle is absolutely huge when it comes to the best way to learn Norwegian, and it has two major applications:

Vocabulary and grammar

The Norwegian language is estimated to be made out of a total of 330000 headwords, whereas the corpus it's built upon contain about 500,000 in total. That's a lot of words!

- The 300 most common words make up 65% of spoken dialogue

- The 1,000 most common words make up 88% of spoken dialogue

So, as you can see, you don't NEED to learn every single last word. Start by focusing on the most common words and the words that are personally going to be useful to you based on your interests and goals.

Just like vocabulary, you want to focus on the most common grammar rules and conjugations (ex. present, preterit, future, conditional, etc.). There are lots of advanced grammar rules that aren't used very often in everyday speech, so they are simply less of a priority.

Learning methods

It seems like there are a million ways to learn Norwegian these days, from traditional methods, like textbooks, to endless online resources. This creates a big problem for language learners: a lack of focus. A lot of people try to dabble in as many as five or six different learning methods and end up spreading themselves too thin.

Instead, **choose the one or two methods that are most effective (giving you 80% of the results)** and ignore the rest. Let's start by outlining some of the methods you could choose for your Norwegian learning.

Popular learning methods

Which methods work, and which ones should you not bother with? Here is a subjective low down.

The reasons why 99% of software and apps won't make you fluent

Take a second and think of all the people you know who learned Norwegian or any second language.

Did any of them become fluent by learning from an app?

Packed with fancy features, there are hundreds of apps and software out there that claim to be the ultimate, game-changing solution to help you learn a language.

- "Advanced speech recognition system!"
- "Adaptive learning algorithm..."
- "Designed by Norwegian scientists."
- "Teaches you a language in just three weeks!"

But do they really work? Is an app really the best way to learn Norwegian?

Or should you file this stuff under the same category as the "Lose 30 pounds in 30 days" diet?

The biggest software and app companies, like Rosetta Stone, Babbel, Busuu, and Duolingo, have all funded their own "independent" studies on the effectiveness of their software. In other words, they all paid the same researcher, who came to the conclusion that every single one of the apps was the best thing since sliced bread.

For example, the study for Babbel concluded:

"...Users need on average 21 hours of study in a two-month period to cover the requirements for one college semester of Norwegian."

This is no surprise because the fill-in-the-blanks, multiple-choice, one-word-at-a-time approach of software is the same kind of stuff you would find on a Norwegian midterm in college.

The problem is that just like software, college and high school Norwegian courses are notorious for teaching students a few basics while leaving them completely unable to actually speak.

At the end of the day, software and apps, just like the traditional courses you take in school, are missing a key ingredient: speaking with real people.

The best and fastest way to learn Norwegian is to spend as much time as possible having real conversations. It's the way that languages have been learned for thousands of years, and although technology can help make this more convenient, it cannot be replaced.

Software companies like Rosetta Stone have finally realized this, and in recent years, they've tried to incorporate some sort of speaking element into their product.

The verdict? Their top review on Amazon was one out of five stars.

Ouch! But if software and apps can't really teach you to speak a language, then why are they so popular?

Because they've turned language learning into a game. Every time you get an answer right, there's a little "beep" that tells you that you did a great job, and soon enough, you are showered with badges, achievements, and cute little cartoons that make it feel like you're really getting it. Of course, these things are also used to guilt you into continuing to use their app. If you stop using them, they start sending you pictures of sad cartoon characters telling you they will die because of your lack of commitment. Really? Do they think we've all turned into four-year-olds?

In the real world, playing this game shields you from the difficult parts of learning a language. You can hide in your room, stare at your phone, and avoid the nervousness that comes with speaking Norwegian in front of a native speaker or the awkward moment when you forget what to say.

But the reality is, every beginner who wants to learn Norwegian will have to face these challenges sooner or later.

The 1% of apps that are actually useful
Despite the drawbacks of software and apps, there is one type of app that can have a profound impact on your learning, and we have been here before:

Electronic flashcards (also known as SRS, or "spaced repetition systems").

I know I have already been over this, but they really do work. Ok, I know they don't sound very glamorous, and maybe the last time you saw a flashcard was in the hands of that nerdy kid in fifth grade that who nobody wanted to sit with at lunchtime.

But please, bear with me because this can totally change the way you learn Norwegian. Here's how a flashcard system works on an app.

Each flashcard will show you an English word, and you have to try and recall the Norwegian word. If you get it wrong, it will show you the card again in one minute, but if you get it right, it will be a longer interval, like 10 minutes or a few days.

A typical basic flashcard app is Anki. (https://apps.ankiweb.net).
Flashcard apps work by repeatedly forcing you to recall words that you struggle to remember, and as you get better, the word shows up less and less frequently. As soon as you feel like you're going to forget a new word, the flashcard will pop up and refresh it.

This system helps you form very strong memories and will allow you to manage a database of all the words you've learned, even those you picked up months or years ago.

You can also use flashcards for grammar concepts. For example, if you're having trouble remembering the conjugations for verbs, just make each conjugation a separate flashcard.

By putting all your conjugations in all the different tenses into flashcards, you now have a way to repeatedly drill them into your memory.

The major advantage of flashcards is that all you really need is 10-20 minutes a day. Every single day, we spend a lot of time waiting around, whether it's for public transportation, in line at the supermarket, or for a doctor's appointment. This is all wasted time that you can use to improve your vocabulary. It only takes a few seconds to turn on the flashcard app and review a few words.

If you want to try this out, these are probably the two best apps out there:

Anki (https://apps.ankiweb.net)
The original, "pure" flashcard app.

Pros:
- Reviewing cards is extremely simple and straightforward.
- Very easy to write your own cards; it can be done on the fly.
- Plenty of customization options and user-written decks to download (although not as many as Memrise).

Cons:

- It can be a bit confusing to set up; you need to be tech-savvy.
- It doesn't provide reminders/motivation to practice daily.

Cost:

- Free for Android, computer.
- US$24.99 for iOS. (At time of writing)

Memrise (https://www.memrise.com)

Flashcard-based app with modern features.

Pros:

- More variety for reviewing cards (fill-in-the-blanks, audio recordings, etc.).
- Offers a little bit of gamification (rewards, reminders) to keep you motivated.
- It has a big library of card decks written by other people and a large community of users.

Cons:

- Writing your own cards (called "Create a Course") is not as easy as Anki and can't be done on mobile.
- The review system works differently from traditional cards.

Cost:

- Free for all platforms (iOS, Android, computer).

Both apps come with standard Norwegian vocabulary decks as well as those written by other users. However, the real beauty of flashcards is being able to write the decks yourself. There is a big advantage to doing this, which you can see from the following steps:

When using pre-written flashcards

- You see a new word for the first time in your app and then review the word until you remember it.

When making flashcards yourself

- You get exposed to a new world through conversation, your teacher, or something you've seen or heard. You associate the word with a real-life situation.
- You write it into a flashcard, and by doing this, you're already strengthening your memory of that word.
- You review the word until you remember it.

As you can see, while making the cards yourself takes a bit of extra work, you get to control the words you learn and can focus on the ones that are more meaningful to you. Plus, the process of writing the word down acts as an extra round of review.

While it is true that flashcard apps have a bit of a learning curve, they are very easy once you get the hang of them, and you'll notice a huge difference in memorizing vocabulary and grammar.

Can you learn Norwegian by just watching TV and listening to the radio?

Countless beginners have tried and failed to learn Norwegian by what is known as "passive listening." Examples of passive listening include:

- Audio courses
- Radio and podcasts
- Movies and TV shows

The idea of passive listening sounds good on paper. You can learn Norwegian by listening to an audio course in your car on the way to work. Put on some Norwegian radio while you're making dinner and then sit down for an episode of *Norsemen* while you fold your laundry.

Except this doesn't work. Why?

Because learning a language is an ACTIVE process. You can't spend hundreds of hours listening to stuff in the background and expect your brain to figure it all out.

Now, many people will have a couple of objections to this:

I thought passive listening is how babies learn languages?

Let's assume out of simplicity that a baby is awake for an average of eight hours a day for the first year of its life. Through all the feedings and diaper changes, it is constantly being exposed to language because its parents are talking to it (and each other). So, by the time a baby says their first words at around the one-year mark, it has already had about three thousand hours of passive-listening exposure (8 hours x 365 days).

Now, how do you compete with that as a busy adult? Even if you squeeze in an hour a day of Norwegian radio into your daily life, it would still take you eight years to get the equivalent amount of language exposure. Who has the patience to spend eight years learning Norwegian?

Don't sell yourself short. With the right method and motivation, you can learn the Norwegian you need in months, not years.

If you incorporate a bit of Norwegian into every aspect of your life, then that's immersion, right? Isn't immersion the best way to learn Norwegian?

There are many expats who have lived in Spain or Latin America for 5-10 years, and guess what? They STILL can't speak a word of Spanish let alone form a sentence.

These people have the perfect environment to learn, they can hear Spanish everywhere when walking down the street, and every friend or acquaintance is someone they can practice with. But somehow, none of this seems to help.

Why?
Because they don't make an effort to speak.

Immersion is extremely effective, but only if you take advantage of the environment you're in and speak Norwegian every chance you get. Simply being there and listening is not enough.

As an adult, we have to learn languages actively. Most of us want to go from beginner to fluent in as short a time as possible, and passive listening is simply too slow.

If you're already listening to a lot of Norwegian, it doesn't mean you should stop. Try to do it actively, which means giving it 100% of your attention rather than having it in the background as you're doing something else.

Listening to radio, TV, and movies can be useful at a later stage. Increasing the amount of Norwegian you hear will speed up your progress when you are already at a conversational level.

But when it comes to learning Norwegian as a complete beginner, there are far more efficient methods.

How to practice Norwegian

We've already established that the best way to learn Norwegian for beginners involves speaking as much as possible. Let's go over the four main ways that you practice speaking Norwegian:

Speak with people you know

Maybe you have friends who are native Norwegian speakers, or maybe you are dating or married to one! If that person is the reason you wanted to learn Norwegian in the first place, it may seem like a good idea to practice with them from the beginning.

Pros:

- It's free.
- Practicing with people you know can be less intimidating than with a stranger, and as a result, you might be more willing to open up and speak (although, for some people, it has the opposite effect).
- They know you, and they like you, so they will probably be very supportive and patient with you.

Cons:

- You may not know anyone in your immediate circle of friends and family who speak Norwegian.
- When you make a mistake, they probably won't be able to explain what you did wrong. Most native speakers don't know the rules of their own language. Things "just sound right" to them.
- People have deeply ingrained habits. Once a relationship is established, it is really hard to change the language of communication. You can try to practice Norwegian with your wife, who is a native speaker, but more often than not, you'll find yourselves defaulting back to English because "it's just easier."
- Trying to practice Norwegian with friends and family can be frustrating. You're going to stutter, you won't

be able to express yourself the way you usually do, and your wonderful sense of humor will suddenly become nonexistent. You'll feel guilty that you're being an inconvenience to them (although most of the time it's a bigger deal for you than it is for them).

Go to Meetups

Norwegian learners often get together a few times a week at a public place (usually a café) and practice speaking for an hour or two. A good place to find them is Meetup.com (https://www.meetup.com). Just do a search for "Norwegian + *the city you live in.*"

Pros:

- It's free.
- You get to meet new people in your area who are learning Norwegian just like you. Since you're all in the same boat, you can encourage each other and help each other stay accountable.
- You can share learning tips with each other, like what's working and what's not.
- If you need an explanation for a grammar concept, chances are someone in the group knows and can explain it to you.

Cons:

- You'll only be able to find meetups in big cities. If you live in a smaller city or town, then you're out of luck.

- It's not great for shy people. Speaking in a group of 10-15 people can be pretty intimidating.
- What often happens at meetups is that you all sit around a table and two or three people will end up doing most of the talking (remember the 80/20 rule?) while the rest just sit there and listen.
- Everyone is at different levels of fluency, so you could find yourself talking to someone who is way more advanced than you are, and you may end up boring them. Unfortunately, some groups don't let complete beginners join for this very reason.
- If you are just starting out and don't feel confident in speaking, you might end up doing a whole lot listening and not much talking. You get much better value out of meetups if you are already somewhat conversational.

Language exchanges

The basic idea is to find a native Norwegian speaker who is trying to learn English. You meet in person or have a Skype call (or something similar) where you split your time practicing both Norwegian and English. The easiest way to find a partner is through online exchanges like My Language Exchange (https://www.mylanguageexchange.com) and Conversation Exchange (https://www.conversationexchange.com).

Pros:

- It's free.

- You can get exposure to a lot of different people who come from different Norwegian-speaking countries and with different backgrounds.

Cons:

- It can be very time consuming to find the right language partner. It can take a lot of trial and error.
- You only get to spend 50% of your time speaking in Norwegian.
- Your partner won't be able to speak English well, so it can be tough to communicate if both of you are beginners.
- Your partner probably won't be able to explain Norwegian grammar to you, and you won't be able to explain English very well, either. For example, can you explain when you should use "which" vs. "that"? Or how about "who" vs. "whom"?
- Partners can be flaky since there is no paid commitment, and some people simply don't show up at the agreed time (happens more often in online exchanges).

Professional Norwegian teachers

These days it is far more convenient to find a Norwegian teacher online, and believe it or not, this can be even more interactive than being face-to-face. You participate in your lessons via Skype from the comfort of home and on your own schedule. This is how many people prefer to learn Norwegian.

Pros:

- A good teacher is like having your own coach or personal trainer. They want you to succeed, and they are there to support you and offer motivation and advice. It is much easier to learn Norwegian when someone is there to hold you accountable.
- A teacher is a trained professional. They have comprehensive knowledge of both Norwegian and English grammar, so they can explain to you the difference between the two, and provide a lot of useful examples to help you understand difficult concepts.
- Teachers know how to correct you when you make a mistake, but not so often as to interrupt the flow of conversation. Talking to a teacher just feels natural.
- Even if you're the shyest person in the world, a good teacher knows how to coax you into speaking and how to build your confidence. You don't have to worry about making mistakes, you'll no longer feel embarrassed, and ultimately, you'll have fun.
- A teacher can quickly figure out your strengths and weaknesses and come up with a learning plan to address them.
- They will design a customized curriculum for you based on your learning goals and interests. This ensures that whatever they teach will be very meaningful to you.
- A good Norwegian teacher should provide you with all the materials that you'll need, so you won't have to

buy a textbook or spend time looking for grammar exercises.

- While a good chunk of your time is spent having conversations, your teacher will introduce exercises that cover all language skills, including pronunciation, reading, writing, and listening.

Cons:

- Just like language exchange partners, it can take some trial and error to find the right teacher. This is true especially if you are looking through an online teacher directory that doesn't do a great job of screening their teachers. You can waste hours scrolling through teacher profiles (which all seem to have five star ratings), only to be disappointed with the one you chose.
- Teachers aren't free. But getting a private teacher is a lot more affordable than you think...

Sure, there are plenty of "high end" teachers who will try to charge you as much as US$60-80/hour. On the "low end," you can probably find someone for less than US$10/hour, although they are usually unqualified tutors who can barely explain things better than your average native speaker.

Verbalicity has a good offer of "high-end" teaching for as little as US$15/hour. You can try out the first lesson for free. Go to: https://verbalicity.com

202 · STEPHEN HERNANDEZ

Of course, there are plenty of people who have learned Norwegian without a teacher. Doing a language exchange or going to a meetup is certainly better than not speaking at all, but it will take much longer to learn, and you may be tempted to give up in the process.

So, if you've got a busy schedule and want to learn Norwegian fast, then getting a teacher is definitely the best way to go.

Road Map: Zero to Conversational

We've just isolated some of the key concepts and methods that make up the best ways to learn Norwegian. Now let's go through the three stages of learning. For each stage, we'll recap what the main goals and recommended method of learning are and offer some more tips on how to progress as quickly as possible.

Stage 1: Introduction

This stage is for absolute beginners. If you already have some knowledge of Norwegian or are used to hearing it, then you can skip to the next stage.

Objective:

The idea is to get a brief introduction to Norwegian with the goal of familiarizing yourself with the following:

- What spoken Norwegian sounds like.
- How it feels to pronounce Norwegian words.

- A few basic phrases.

This helps you acclimatize to learning a new language and gets you used to listening and speaking right away.

After this stage, you probably will have some basic phrases under your belt, like "My name is…", "Where are you from?" and "What time is it?"

How to do it:

Start with a free audio course or one of the popular apps. Ideally, it should be a guided course that's easy to follow. Here are some examples:

- 17 Minute Languages audio course, Google Play: Learn Norwegian Free.
- Get Memrise (https://www.memrise.com) and start using their basic Norwegian course, or use other free apps like Duolingo (https://www.duolingo.com).

"Wait," you are no doubt be saying to yourself, "didn't he say that apps can't teach you a language?"

That's true. But I didn't say they couldn't help, and at this point in time, all you're trying to do is get your bearings and get comfortable with listening and repeating.

You probably only need about 30 minutes a day, and this introductory stage should last no more than a few weeks.

Afterward, you can cut down or stop using these resources altogether because, although they are fine as an introduction, they are slow and inefficient. You should move on to better options, which we'll cover next.

Tip for this stage:

Focus on pronunciation

Try to get your pronunciation right from the very beginning. When you hear the Norwegian recording, make sure you repeat it out loud.

At first, repeat each word slowly, syllable by syllable, until you can mimic the sounds almost perfectly. If necessary, record yourself speaking and listen back.

Once you're satisfied that you're saying it right, then repeat it over and over again until it feels natural.

Stage 2: Beginner

Objective:

At this stage, the goal is to build a solid foundation for yourself in terms of basic grammar and vocabulary, put your thoughts into complete sentences, and be confident enough to talk to people.

At the end of this stage, you want to be able to have basic conversations that involve exchanging information, asking for things, and talking about work, family, and your interests.

Effectively, you want to be at an upper-beginner level.

How to do it:
For the beginner stage, the best way to learn Norwegian is to choose one of these two options:

Option 1:
- Textbook
- Speaking practice: friends, meetups, exchanges, Skype.
- Flashcards (optional)

Using a textbook might seem old-fashioned, but it is still probably the best way for a beginner to learn the grammatical rules of Norwegian. The reason why a textbook is effective is that it teaches you in a structured way. It takes you through a progression that slowly builds on each concept, step by step.

For each chapter of the textbook that you go through, study the dialogues and make sure you do all the practice exercises. Ideally, you should try to find additional exercises online related to the concept you just learned.

Just like most forms of learning, a textbook can't actually teach you to speak. So, for each concept you learn, you need to be practicing it with real people.

206 · STEPHEN HERNANDEZ

You can use a combination of friends, meetups, or language exchanges to get your practice in. At this point, you are not having full conversations yet (nor should you try to). Try practicing phrases and some short dialogues or scenarios. But nevertheless, you should aim for one to two hours per week of speaking practice.

Option 2:

- Learn with a Norwegian teacher in person or online
- Flashcards (optional)

When you learn with a teacher, you get step-by-step guidance and speaking practice all in one package.

A good Norwegian teacher will send or give you textbook materials and all the practice exercises you'll ever need, so there is no need to look for materials on your own. You even get homework, just like in school.

A teacher can also explain grammar to you in different ways and answer your questions if you don't understand. This is a big advantage over someone who is just studying on their own.

Being able to practice what you learned immediately through speaking is another advantage. For example, you might spend the first half of a lesson going over the conjugations of the Imperfect tense and then spend the second half the lesson practicing it verbally through question and answer, storytelling, and other fun exercises.

Flashcards

It is never too early to start using flashcards to help you remember words.

But especially if you've chosen Option 1, it might be a little overwhelming to be studying while trying to find practice opportunities, and you don't want to add another method like flashcards to distract you from that.

Remember the 80/20 rule. It is better to focus on a few things that have the highest impact.

But if you feel like you're having trouble remembering new words or grammar conjugations, then it's probably time to incorporate flashcards into your routine.

Tips for this stage:

Don't jump ahead

It might be tempting to immediately work your way through a textbook from cover to cover, but this will just overload you with information.

A lot of people make the mistake of diving too deep into the grammar without making sure that they fully understand and have practiced each concept before moving on to the next. If in doubt, spend more time reviewing what you've already learned.

Be strategic about your vocabulary

Focus on memorizing the most useful words that will make it easier for you to practice speaking. Highly useful words include "power verbs" and "connectors." You can find these online or in any decent text book

If you master these types of words, your speech will come out more naturally, and it will make you sound more fluent than you actually are at this point. This can give you a much-needed boost of confidence because, at this stage, it can still be scary to be out there talking to people.

Intermediate

Objective:

This stage is all about expanding your horizons. It's about greatly increasing your vocabulary, comprehension skills, and confidence in using Norwegian in a variety of situations.

At the end of this stage, you want to be able to express yourself freely and talk about different topics, like what's happening in the news, your hopes and dreams, or your opinion on a particular subject.

You're still going to make plenty of mistakes, and your grammar won't be perfect, but the goal is to be able to get your ideas across, whatever they may be. If you can do that, you'll reach the upper intermediate level and be considered **conversationally fluent**.

Some may choose to improve their Norwegian even further, to more advanced levels, but for many people, this is this level where you can fully enjoy the rewards of being able to speak Norwegian.

How to do it:

Based on the two options from the beginner stage, we can make a few adjustments for the intermediate level:
Option 1:

- Speaking practice (*friends, meetups, exchanges*)
- Reading and listening
- Flashcards
- Textbooks (*optional*)

Option 2:

- Learn with a Norwegian teacher
- Reading and listening
- Flashcards

Speaking practice

To move into the intermediate stage, speaking becomes even more important. By now you should be ramping up your speaking practice to a **minimum of two to three hours per week**.

Whereas you were previously practicing short phrases or dialogues, you should now be able to have more full-fledged conversations because you know more vocabulary and grammar.

If you are learning with a teacher, you should know them pretty well by now, so you can have deeper conversations about more diverse topics. Your teacher can also start to speak a little bit faster to help train your ear.

Active Reading/Listening

This is the stage where active reading and listening start to shine. You know enough Norwegian now that you can really take advantage of movies, TV, radio, podcasts, books, and articles.

You won't understand 100% of what you read and hear. Heck, maybe you only understand 50-60% at this point, but that is enough to get the gist of what is going on. If you're watching TV shows or movies, turn on Norwegian subtitles (Netflix is great for this). Reading and listening at the same time will get you the best results.

Try to find material that is interesting to you. This way, you can enjoy the process of listening and reading, which can become a source of motivation. You'll also pick up Norwegian that is relevant and useful to you personally.

Remember, "Active" means giving it your full attention. Try your best to understand it and pay attention to the grammar and vocabulary and the context in which they are being used. If there is anything you don't understand, write it down so you can look it up later, or ask your teacher during your next lesson.

Flashcards

A big part of going from beginner to intermediate is significantly increasing your vocabulary. By now, you will have already learned all the "easy" words, and to further build your vocabulary, you need to be very deliberate about remembering all the new words you are exposed to every day. Using flashcard apps like Anki or Memrise can really help commit them to memory. You can practice in five-minute chunks (while waiting for the bus, etc.) for a total of 10-20 minutes a day to get great results.

Textbook

A textbook is not mandatory at this point. You've learned most of the important grammar, and now the focus should be to practice it until you can use it fluidly.

Of course, there are always more advanced grammar concepts to learn, but they tend to be used very sparingly in everyday conversations.

Tips for this stage:

Learning formula

Your "routine" for learning new material should look something like this:

- You're exposed to new Norwegian vocabulary and grammar through your teacher and textbook or by listening and reading.
- Review it using flashcards.
- Speak it until it becomes second nature.

For example, you hear a phrase on a Norwegian TV show which you are not familiar with.

You look up the meaning and then create a new flashcard in Anki.

The next day, the flashcard pops up, and you review it.

A few days later, you head to your Norwegian meetup, and during a conversation bring up the phrase

Staying Motivated

When you reach the intermediate stage, you may feel like you're not progressing as fast as you did before. In fact, there will be times where you feel like you aren't improving at all.

This is the classic "dip" that comes with learning any skill, and Norwegian is no exception.

This happens because you've already learned a lot of the "low-hanging fruit." What you are learning now is more incremental and takes longer for everything to click in your mind.

To overcome the dip, you need to trust the process and be disciplined when it comes to the learning formula.

Your teacher can really help you stay motivated by creating a plan that guides you to new things you should learn and older concepts you should be reviewing, as well as giving you feedback on what you are doing well and what you need to improve on.

Time Frame

So, how long does it take to learn Norwegian using this road map?

I'm not going to lie to you and say that you can become fluent in 30 days. Maybe some people can, but most of us lead busy lives, with jobs, families, and other responsibilities competing for our time.

If you are learning with a Norwegian teacher (Option 2), I believe that you can go from zero to conversationally fluent in **8–12 months** using the methods in this road map.

This assumes that you can spend **one hour per day** working on your Norwegian, whether that's the actual Norwegian lessons themselves, reviewing flashcards, or actively listening and reading.

This timeframe is just an estimate because, obviously, everyone learns at a different pace. Of course, the more time you dedicate to learning Norwegian, the faster you'll progress.

If you decide to go at it alone (Option 1), it will take a lot longer. But if you follow the best way to learn Norwegian as outlined in the road map, stay disciplined, and make sure you consistently get enough conversation practice, you'll get there eventually.

Final Thoughts

Absolutely anyone can learn Norwegian.

It doesn't matter whether or not you have a talent for languages or whether you are a naturally fast learner.

At the end of the day, learning Norwegian is about motivation, focus, and time.

If you've got all three of these things and you commit to speaking rather than just learning the "stuff" of Norwegian, then you simply cannot fail.

And of course, don't forget to have FUN! The process should be as enjoyable as the end goal.

CHAPTER FIFTEEN

LEARNING WITHOUT TRYING

Remember the story about the lazy bricklayer way back in Chapter One? Well, to recap, the lazy way, or the way that involves the least amount of work, is most often the smartest way to do things.

Do the things that involve the least amount of work when learning a language. Engage in effortless language learning, not completely effortless, of course, but as effortless as possible.

The word "effortless" in this context is borrowed from two sources. One is AJ Hoge, who is a great teacher of English. His channel and website are both called Effortless English. The other source is Taoist philosophy.

Effortlessness and the Parable of the Crooked Tree

When the linguist Steve Kaufmann (who, incidentally, can speak over 20 languages) wrote his book *The Linguist: A Personal Guide to Language Learning*, he began with what he called "The Parable of the Crooked Tree."

The author of the parable was Zhuangzi, an early exponent of Taoism, a school of Chinese philosophy from over two thousand years ago. Zhuangzi's basic principle in life was to follow what was natural, what was effortless, and not try to force things.

Typically, the Taoist philosophy was in opposition to Confucianism, which prescribed rules of what you should and shouldn't do to be a great person. Confucianism is full of admonishments on how you should behave. As is often the case with prescriptive philosophies or religions, these "commandments" attempt to set the boundaries of correct behavior. Zhuangzi was different. He advised people to follow their own natures and to not resist the world around them. This effortless non-resistance would help them learn better and be happier.

In Zhuangzi's parable of the crooked tree, his friend Huizi tells him that a tree they are both observing is crooked because the lumber is not good for anything, like Zhuangzi's philosophy.

"Neither your philosophy nor the tree is good for anything," says Huizi.

Zhuangzi replies, "You say that because you don't know how to use them. You have to use things for the purpose intended and understand their true nature. You can sit underneath a crooked tree and enjoy its shade, for example. If you understand the true nature of things, you will be able to use them to achieve your goals."

I'm in the lumber business, and sometimes those gnarly old trees produce very expensive and decorative wood. Compared to trees in a planted forest, their wood is less uniform and less suitable for industrial end uses. We just have to accept these more individualistic trees as they are and appreciate what they bring. Zhuangzi defends his philosophy, saying it is useful if we accept its nature and know how to use it.

Zhuangi's philosophy was based on effortlessness, "wu wei" (无为) in Chinese. In other words, if you want to learn better, stop resisting; go with the flow. That has always been my approach. Language learning does require some effort, of course, but we learn best when effort is minimized and pleasure is maximized.

Let's look at something that requires effort but is also usually enjoyable: reading.

If you are reading in a language that you read well and you come across a few unknown words, you usually don't look up those unknown words in a dictionary because it's too much trouble and you have usually worked out the meaning because of the context.

So, what happens if you are reading something in Norwegian as a beginner and have to constantly resort to dictionaries? They are no longer the learning aid they once were but become a chore and a block to enjoying reading in the way you are accustomed. And what's worse, if you don't memorize these new words' meanings, you will keep on getting bogged down. So, is there a better or easier way to start off reading in Norwegian - an effortless way?

Thankfully, yes, there is. It is called LingQ (https://www.lingq.com/en). You can read in Norwegian using LingQ on your computer, laptop, iPad, or smartphone.

When you look up a word in LingQ, it's highlighted. The word then appears highlighted in any subsequent material so you are reminded that you've looked it up before. You can see the meaning straight away, and eventually it becomes part of you, without any effort.

You are not just looking words up in a dictionary and then forgetting them. You are creating your own personal database of words and phrases for easy review as you continue reading.

Steve Kaufmann highly recommends this as a way of learning a language, and he should know. He has similar practical thoughts on grammar:

When I read grammar – and I believe we should occasionally read grammar rules as it helps give us a sense of the language – I don't try to remember anything.

I don't try to learn or understand anything. I just treat it as a spark, an exposure of something that might help me eventually get a sense of the language. I don't worry about grammar. I know it will gradually become clearer for me.

Have you ever noticed how some people can learn languages effortlessly (Steve Kaufmann would be one), getting to fluency faster with pen and paper than others do with a bag full of textbooks and phone-full of learning apps?

Everything about their learning seems effortless, and every new word and expression they learn is used with utmost confidence.

What is it about these individuals that sets them apart?

Every language learner strives for this effortlessly cool way of learning, where study ceases to be a chore and language usage becomes commonplace.

While it may seem like these individuals were born with a natural linguistic talent, it actually all comes down to a few simple habits these super-learners integrate into their daily life.

Here's a short list, along with some tips on implementing these habits in your daily life and becoming the confident speaker you want to be.

Note: You do not have to follow these recommendations exactly; adapt them to your lifestyle and unique personality.

Review before learning, even if it means you don't have time or energy to learn more.

Effective language learners know that what you don't review, you forget forever, and forgetting means that all that time you've spent learning the new word or expression has been put to waste.

That is why you should always prioritize reviewing above learning and start every study session by going over your past notes and flashcards.

That way, if you realize halfway through that you're just too exhausted to make the progress you hoped for, you've at least made sure you don't regress by activating all the connections already in your brain!

Tip: Never learn something new before you review what you know already.

Study a little bit every day and don't mistake the illusion of progress for actual improvement.

Effective language learners understand that binge-learning is but an illusion of progress.

When you try to learn long lists of vocabulary all at once or leaf through a textbook, chapter after chapter, without giving the necessary thought to the information within, your brain starts a tally that addictively goes up with every leaf.

The problem is, that mental counter represents the number of words and lessons you've seen, not the information you can actually use, or even remember the next morning.

Binge learning is extremely motivating at the beginning, but it consistently leads to burnout when the rational part of your brain finally realizes that all this euphoria was, in fact, unjustified.

Tip: Study in small chunks every day, even if for just five or 10 minutes.

Have a clear goal and use the language for something you already enjoy.

Effective learners realize that you can't learn a language without motivation that comes from the prospect of using it in the context you're passionate about.

For example: If you love horses, include equestrian themes throughout your learning. If you enjoy scuba diving like me, include Norwegian-speaking scuba-diving sites in your learning.

Tip: Use the language in the context of the topics you're passionate about and the activities you enjoy.

Avoid having a closet full of unopened textbooks or a phone full of learning apps.

Effective language learners know that there's no silver bullet to language learning, so they don't waste time searching for it. They choose an effective method quickly and stick to it until there is a real need to change.

One mistake beginners in language learning fall victim to again and again is going on a shopping spree for learning resources only to realize that they are spending more time scavenging for new ways to learn than actually learning.

It's good to choose a methodology that works for you, but it's even more important to do so quickly and get back to learning.

Tip: Spend a week researching different learning methods, select one or two that suit you best, and stick with them until you've read them cover to cover or identify a clear need to supplement them with another resource.

Strike a balance between consuming the language and using it to convey your thoughts.

Effective learners value output as much as input and make sure to write or say a new word out loud every time they read or listen to one.

There are countless examples of language learners who spend all their time cramming vocabulary only to find themselves at a loss for words when thrown into a real-life conversation.

There are also countless examples of those who dedicate every minute to speaking to friends and blogging in the target language. Such students are often remarkably fluent in their specific topic of interest or when they speak to their usual interlocutors, but they can struggle to produce a single coherent sentence outside of that context.

No matter your ultimate goal, it is crucial to learn languages in a balanced way. Reading and listening to native material on a diverse range of topics will enrich your own expressiveness. Using new words and expressions you've picked up from others will cement them in your memory.

Tip: Dedicate as much time to speaking and writing as to reading and listening and try to regularly wander into topics outside your comfort zone.

You will often fail, so celebrate your mistakes as opportunities to get better.

Effective learners value mistakes and misunderstandings as opportunities to learn and improve.

Everyone remembers Henry Ford's Model T, but what preceded it was a very imperfect Model A. Ford's mechanics gathered real-world insight into all its deficiencies and fixed them one at a time before coming up with the icon of the automotive history.

The only way to improve is to start using new expressions right after you learn them, make mistakes, and use those mistakes to improve your abilities.

It's not a failure to use the wrong grammar or make a blatant spelling mistake. The only true failure is when you don't learn from the mess-up or use it as an excuse to give up.

Tip: Don't look at mistakes as failures but rather as immediate opportunities to improve your language abilities.

Always be attentive and try to imitate the way native speakers use the language.

Effective learners mimic what expressions native speakers use in a given context, how they pronounce them, and what gestures they choose to reinforce their message.

Textbooks and dictionaries are great at teaching you what's grammatically correct, but they can't guide you to speak naturally in day-to-day situations. An expression that would give you full marks on a test, and pass every spell check, may sound absolutely jarring in the real world.

The best way to learn the language as it is actually spoken is to put yourself in context with native speakers and listen carefully to what they say! Then note down the natural sentence patterns you hear and use them yourself.

Next time you're queuing up for a matcha latte, stop trying to imagine the conversation you'll have with the barista and instead listen to the conversations she's having with other clients!

Tip: Always be attentive to what native speakers say in any given situation and note down the sentence patterns they use.

Let's leave this chapter by just recapping some of the major points made throughout this book:

- Something inside you has got to want to learn the language.
- Ignore grammar at the beginning and concentrate instead on learning new words.
- Work on learning the most commonly used words and forget about words that are rarely ever used.
- Make language learning automatic by listening, reading, and digesting the language wherever you can.
- And finally, find ways to make learning fun by reading new books, subscribing to blogs, translating street signs, listening to music, or conversing with strangers.

I leave you with the immortal words of Fatboy Slim: *"Just lay back and let the big beat lead you."*

CONCLUSION

If you have learned one thing from this book, I hope it is that the most effective learning is not obtained by trying too hard. If you fill your head with useless vocabulary and grammar rules you do not need to speak Norwegian, eventually you will burn out and give up. Just keep to the bare minimum when starting out, find what works for you, and stick with that until something more effective comes your way.

You will have gathered by now that learning to speak Norwegian is different from just learning Norwegian. The emphasis is always on speaking. and understanding.

Learn at your own pace; do not force it. Find your own way. It is better to go slowly but surely rather than rush. The tortoise will always do better than the hare in language learning.

My abiding hope is that by the end of this book, you will have found your own path to speaking Norwegian fluently and effortlessly.

Lykke til!

BIBLIOGRAPHY / ONLINE RESOURCES

I have literally begged, borrowed, or stolen a lot of the content of this book, and I am indebted to the authors, teachers, website owners, app writers, and bloggers who have spent valuable time putting resources online or in print to help people learn a new language. I will list them after this brief epilogue.

I urge you to use the resources they have made available. Find what works for you. It may be a combination of all or some of them, or even just one. If you can't afford to buy their stuff, use the free stuff until you can. It will be well worth it.

By the way, I do not receive any sort of commission or kickback for recommending any of the courses, websites, blogs, or apps mentioned throughout this book. The fact that I have included them is based purely on merit. Any of these *helpers* will stand you in good stead.

I was lucky. I started learning new languages when I was young, sometimes out of necessity (just to be understood by my peers) and sometimes out of precocious curiosity. I was also - and still am - filled with wanderlust and spent my mid- and late-teenage years hitchhiking around Europe (without a penny to my name and devoid of any dictionary, travel guide, or even map). "Ah," I hear you say, "that's why it was so easy for you, but I'm an adult, and I have a million things on my mind and a trillion things to do. It's so easy when you are a kid. You don't have to worry about anything else apart from living. I have so many responsibilities."

Yes and no. Kids do worry about a spectacular amount of things, and a lot of their time is tied up with doing things they also consider important. What makes the difference with learning like a child is that children learn or assimilate a language faster because, one, they have fewer hang-ups about making mistakes and interacting with other language speakers, and two, they learn better when they are having fun and are interested. This is when they are seemingly picking up the language effortlessly.

My aim is to rekindle some of that emotion in you. Stick your thumb in the air, hitch a lift from whatever resource gets you moving, sit back, and enjoy the ride. Make this journey fun and exciting, and you will speak Norwegian at the end of it.

- Anki (https://apps.ankiweb.net/) SRS (spaced repetition software) with intelligent flashcards.
- Dagbladet (https://www.dagbladet.no/) Online Norwegian newspaper.
- CoffeeBreak Norwegian (https://radiolingua.com/) Learn Norwegian on your coffee break.
- ConversationExchange (https://www.conversationexchange.com) Practice with native speakers in your area.
- Duolingo (https://www.duolingo.com/) Fun podcast for learning Norwegian.

- FluentU (https://www.fluentu.com/en/) SRS app and language immersion online.
- Norwegian Pod 101 (https://www.Norwegianpod101.com/) Podcast for real beginners.
- italki (https://www.italki.com/) Online teaching and conversation resource.
- Languages-Direct (https://www.languages-direct.com/) Norwegian printed and audio materials audio magazine.
- LingQ (https://www.lingq.com/en/) Online reading resource.
- Meetup (https://www.meetup.com/) Online language exchange.
- Memrise (https://www.memrise.com/) Memory techniques to speed up language learning.
- My Language Exchange (mylanguageexchange.com) Online language exchange community.
- Learn Norwegian II Norwegian/English Parallel Texts.
- stephenhernandez.co.uk (https://stephenhernandez.co.uk/) Free tips on how to improve your language learning.
- SuperMemo (https://www.supermemo.com/en) SRS app.
- The Intrepid Guide Survival Norwegian travel phrase guide with pronunciation.
- The Positivity Blog (https://www.positivityblog.com/) Henrik Edberg's positivity blog.
- Verbalicity (https://verbalicity.com/) One-on-one online lessons with native teachers.

Made in the USA
Columbia, SC
15 May 2023

16764369R00126